'AT THE END
OF THE DAY,
YOUR FEET SHOULD
BE DIRTY, YOUR HAIR
MESSY AND YOUR
EYES SPARKLING'
SHANTI

THE WILD BOOK

OUTDOOR ACTIVITIES TO UNLEASH YOUR INNER CHILD

DAVID SCARFE

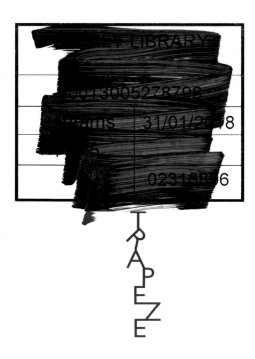

CONTENTS

CONTENTS

'Wildness is a necessity'

JOHN MUIR

Each day it gets just a little bit harder to be wild. Children are better at it. Your childhood probably brings back memories of climbing trees, collecting insects, jumping in puddles and running through fields. Wildness was in your veins then. As we get older, though, these things fall away and with them we lose the wild spirit that once made us feel so alive.

Now, more than ever, when the first and last thing we do each day is to check our smartphones, with little time in between spent noticing the world around us, we need some wildness in our lives.

This book came about because of that need. Having been born in a city and spending much of my life since cooped up in an office, I wondered how I could ever re-connect with the world out there. Like so many people, I would fantasise about leaving everything behind to go on a great adventure, but the truth is that wildness is much closer than that. We just need a little encouragement.

And so, I began to re-learn things that I had once known but since forgotten. I began to give myself a reason to go outside and try new things, rather than staying in and watching that TV programme again. To go for a walk with friends, rather than driving to the movies. To learn how to find food and drink in the wild, rather than doing an online shop. Wildness is on our doorstep, if we are willing to cross the threshold.

This is not a survivalist guide – there are countless, expert books on that subject – but it is in its own way about staying alive. Because wildness is really another word for living, in its truest sense. The smallest interactions with nature can make us feel alive to the world around us and as we get to know the wild we truly get to know something of ourselves too.

I hope this book will bring the reader as much pleasure as it has brought me putting it together.

Let a little wildness in. You won't regret it.

The Author, 2017

MIDSUMMER FLOWER CROWN

'Find beauty not only in the thing itself, but in the pattern of the shadows, the light and dark which that thing provides'

JUNICHIRO TANIZAKI

The Ancient Greeks wore wreaths made from different plants, depending on which god they wanted to cosy up to: oak for Zeus, laurel for Apollo, grapevines for the god of booze, Dionysus, and myrtle for Aphrodite, goddess of love. Nowadays, we associate wreaths more with festive celebrations than we do with holy days.

The Swedish Flower Crown was originally part of an ancient fertility festival but is now worn at Midsummer, the most important holiday in the country's calendar.

YOU WILL NEED
- A variety of fresh flowers trimmed down to 3-inch stems
- 2 pieces of floral cloth wire
- Green floral tape
- Floral shears or a strong pair of scissors

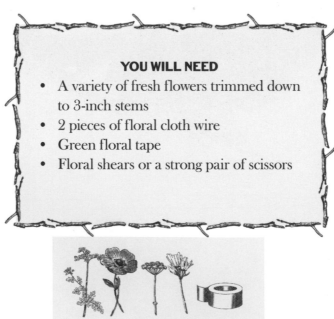

First, you need to create the base of the crown using the two pieces of floral wire. Gently bend each piece into a semicircle and place the two halves to form a circle. Lay it on top of your head to check the size is correct.

You want it to fit snugly, as once the flowers are in place it's going to be quite heavy. When you have the right size, join the two overlapping sections of wire tightly together using the floral tape.

Before you add any flowers to the base, you need to create several small bunches of flowers. Each bunch should be made up of 4 or 5 flowers, nestled one beneath the other.

When ready, tightly wrap the base of each bunch with floral tape. If necessary, trim the tips to an even length.

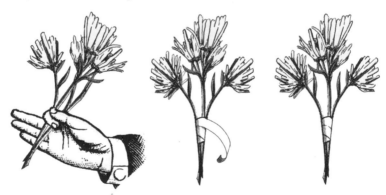

Once you have made ten or so bunches, begin joining them to the base. With the floral tape, tightly wrap each bunch to the outside of the wire base. Each new cluster you add should overlap with the last one. Continue in the same direction until the crown is complete.

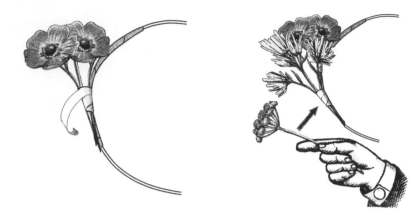

If you are not going to wear the crown immediately, then you can spray it with water and store it somewhere cool to help it last longer.

MUDLARKING

'The Thames is the repository and guardian of London's
undiscovered treasures' **JANE SHILLING**

F ar from being hobbyists, the original 'mudlarks' were among the poorest
of the poor of 18th-century London. Unfortunate people (many of them
children) would trawl the banks of the Thames at low tide in search of coal,
bones, driftwood or anything of the least value.

It was a pitiful task. The Thames at that time was the city's rubbish dump,
awash with raw sewage as well as the corpses of dogs, cats and humans, and
the mudlarks were at constant risk of infection from objects sunk into the
mud.

Nowadays, though, mudlarking has undergone a complete transformation
from its inauspicious origins. Many river beaches around the world (including
the rejuvenated Thames) have become a draw for amateur archaeologists and
all those seeking a window into our past.

CHOOSING A LOCATION

Before you set out, you will need to know the local tide tables and any other
safety information. Be sure to visit your local authority's website to find out
what is required before you go beachcombing.

Depending on where you are looking, you may also
need to get a licence.

KNOWING WHAT TO LOOK FOR

If you are searching the banks of a fast-flowing river then you may find that the beach's surface has been washed clean of any artefacts. Pebbled areas are harder to search. Instead, look for patches of clay, where the river bed is exposed.

The tide will naturally group similar items together, so if you find pieces of scrap metal somewhere then keep searching as you are likely to find more interesting metal there.

HOW TO SEARCH

You don't need a metal detector to go mudlarking – some authorities will require a special permit for you to do so and may even prohibit them altogether.

Instead, the beachcomber's single most important piece of kit is the trowel – the kind that a bricklayer would use for pointing. Use this to delicately sift through the surface materials of stones, grit and lumps of compacted clay. Depending where you are, the rules may dictate that you don't actually dig up the riverbank but instead scrape lightly to search.

FINDING TREASURE

Most beachcombers are looking for valuable metal, though there are beautiful natural objects on show such as pebbles and shells. Indeed humble pebbles found on the banks of the Thames are likely to have been deposited by glaciers during the last Ice Age, 21,000 years ago.

Take the magpie approach: anything that has been preserved in the mud will appear shiny, as it will have been protected from rust. If you are searching the Thames then you are in with a good chance of finding clay tobacco pipes dating from the 17th and 18th centuries, which were manufactured along the foreshore.

Medieval pins are not uncommon, and you might strike it lucky and find an antique coin.

A JOURNEY OF DISCOVERY

Mudlarking doesn't end at the beach. In a good day's scouring you would aim to fill a small bucket with interesting items. Your task is then to discover whatever you can about them.

Internet research can point you in the right direction but local museums may be able to offer expert help and, depending on how exciting your finds are, they might even encourage you to register your finds with them.

CLOUDSPOTTING

'When I do not walk in the clouds I walk as though I were lost'
ANTONIO PORCHIA

For what are essentially vast collections of water drops, clouds have a profoundly mystic, as well as a psychoanalytic, power to them. We have all at one time gazed upwards and felt the deep sense of calm that comes from watching a fluffy white cumulus migrate silently across the endless blue. There is, though, a huge array of clouds and a study of each different type and knowing what they mean can make your daydreaming glance at the heavens that much more meaningful.

There are ten basic types of cloud, which are grouped according to their appearance – whether they are made up of layers, streaks or individual clumps – as well as how high they are. These ten types are then subdivided into a host of species and varieties.

Below are just a few of the vast range of different types of cloud, some of which are common and easy to spot, and some rare. There is nothing so changeable as the weather and you never know when an interesting formation is going to appear, so be vigilant.

CUMULUS

Cumulus are the cotton-wool puffs beloved of Pixar and lazy watercolour painters everywhere. They have flat bases and cauliflower tops and typically slide gently across the sky during sunny days. Usually they form just a few hours after dawn and tend to dissipate before sunset.

Cumulus form on top of columns of air, known as thermals, which rise from the ground as it gets heated by the sun. Most cumulus begin to break down at the grand old age of about 15 minutes, after which point their edges start to fray and they become known as cumulus fractus.

Smaller cumulus will not bring rain or snow but larger clouds can create light to moderate showers. There is an old saying that as cumuli build upwards in the morning they presage heavy showers later on: 'In the morning mountains, in the afternoon fountains'.

STRATOCUMULUS

This is the most common of all the cloud types in the UK, as well as many other parts of the world. Stratocumulus is a lower-forming patch of cloud with a clumpy base. These patches are either joined up, or have spaces in between them. Typically, a sky filled with stratocumulus appears overcast, with low-looking clouds made up of white to dark grey tones.

Stratocumulus can sometimes bring rain or snow, but usually it will be light. Their normal contribution is to block out any chance of sunshine and ruin bank-holiday weekends. They often become more plentiful during the morning, spreading to a wide net of cloud reaching across the sky.

CUMULONIMBUS

Now we're talking. Cumulonimbus has been described as the 'King of Clouds' by overexcited weathermen. It is a spectacular-looking, atmospheric driving force of a cloud.

This vast storm cloud can spread upwards over 10 miles into the sky, its upper reaches forming a huge canopy of ice crystals that looks something like a great blacksmith's anvil from a distance. As seen from below, however, cumulonimbus looks like a forbiddingly dark, ragged cloud drawn across the sky.

Cumulonimbus are the storm clouds. They are bringers of heavy rain, snow and even hailstones, as well as thunder and lightning. As opposed to the dark, featureless nimbostratus that produces prolonged, continuous rain (and which never gets invited to parties), cumulonimbus delivers its payload of weather in sudden, dramatic downpours.

Aircraft pilots will avoid cumulonimbus like the plague. Indeed, powerful up-and-down draughts have been known to flip an aircraft upside down (not to mention spill your Bloody Mary in the process).

ALTOCUMULUS

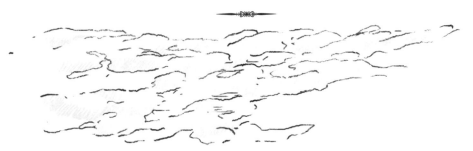

This mid-level cloud is the connoisseur's choice. Forming in layers of individual rolls of cloud, from beneath they look like beautiful ridges of fluffy white cotton wool that appear especially magnificent when backlit by the burnt umber of a sunset.

Altocumulus is not to be confused with the similar-looking cirrocumulus, which is composed of smaller cloudlets. To tell them apart, hold a finger at arm's length towards the sky: if the cloudlets are smaller than the width of your finger they are cirrocumulus; if not, you have got yourself an altocumulus.

Rain and snow produced by an altocumulus will not usually reach ground level. However, to the keenly trained eye of a cloudspotter, these clouds can be early indicators of storms ahead. Their bumpy tops are the result of an unstable atmosphere, which means that they are likely to form into cumulonimbus.

CIRRUS

Arguably the most beautiful of the major cloud types, cirrus appear as delicate streaks of white against an azure sky. Named after the Latin for 'a lock of hair', they are typically translucent and made up of ice crystals cascading through the high atmosphere.

As these ice crystals fall, they travel through different atmospheric regions and variously drier, moister, faster and slower patches of air. This effect gives the cloud its trademark wavy strokes, known as 'fallstreaks'.

These ice crystals evaporate as they fall and so never reach the ground. If lots of cirrus appear to join together and thicken to form the high layer cloud cirrostratus, this can be an early sign of coming rain.

LENTICULARIS

Taking their name from the Latin for 'lentil' (though we think that had the Romans known about disposable contact lenses they might have opted for that instead), lenticularis are discs of cloud, formed with smooth edges.

They form in stable conditions, when moist winds are forced upwards by rising ground, such as a mountain. For this reason, they are usually found in mountainous regions, though they can also form downwind of a gentler, rolling hillside if conditions allow.

Though they appear blissfully calm and motionless from a distance, lenticularis are made up of a great rush of water droplets carried on the wind from one side of the cloud to the other.

MAMMA

Mamma are the pockets that hang beneath cloud layers. They can be best seen when the sun is low and casting light across the base of the cloud layer. Mamma comes from the Latin for 'udders' and, as you will discover, it is a well-chosen name.

They are a rewarding find for the cloudspotter, given their relative rarity, and look most dramatic when they form on the underside of the giant anvils of cumulonimbus storm clouds.

Usually, mamma are found attached to the rear of an advancing storm front. So, if you can see them, chances are that you are on the good side of bad weather.

NOCTILUCENT

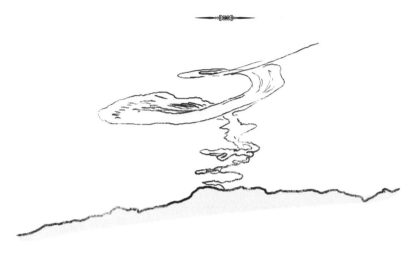

Noctilucent clouds form so much higher than 'normal' weather clouds that they might almost be counted as another species – they form around 50 miles up, as opposed to the usual 10–12 miles.

These rather uncanny clouds have a disquieting feel about them; a blue-white, almost spectral colouring that can often appear in the form of delicate ripples spread across a vast swathe of sky. They are so called because they shine; being so high up, they catch the last rays of the sinking sun when all else is dark, giving them a strangely out-of-time feel.

Ghosts that they are, noctilucent travel far too high in the sky to affect weather on the ground (though interestingly they are increasingly considered harbingers of climate change).

Noctilucent are rare, only forming in the summer months, usually between the end of May and middle of August. They are best seen within a few hours of sunset or sunrise, when the light is changing and the sky is clear of any lower clouds.

STARGAZING

'I know nothing with any certainty, but the sight of the stars makes me dream'

VINCENT VAN GOGH

As far as taking up new hobbies goes, Stargazing might seem about as forbidding as it gets: after all, there is a potentially infinite universe out there to be deciphered. There are, though, some simple ways by which you can begin to learn the night sky and once you have a basic grasp of the essentials you will be able to unlock the most wondrous and awe-inspiring spectacle that it is possible for the human eye to look upon.

The first step is to look up. Obvious as that might sound, stargazing is about getting into the habit of noticing the night sky and familiarising yourself with the bright objects and patterns drawn among the stars.

A good idea is to start with the Moon. Earth's companion moon can be seen from almost everywhere – crowded city streets, open fields, through the window of a No. 73 bus – and the moon's orbit of the earth is regular and predictable.

Try to observe it at the same time each night. What do you see? Is it closer or further? How much of it is visible?

Like Earth, the Moon is always half-illuminated by our sun, and has a day-side and a night-side. From our vantage point on the ground, we see varying fractions of both its day and night sides, which are known as 'phases'.

These phases depend on where the Moon is in respect to the sun in space. (You may be getting flashbacks to school science lessons at this point.)

During a full moon, for instance, the Sun, the Earth and the Moon are all aligned, with Earth in the middle. The Moon's fully illuminated 'day' side faces the Earth's 'night' side – hence why we get such a spectacular view.

So, whenever you look at the Moon, consider where the Sun is and that will help you to understand why the moon is in a particular phase.

The next important thing to know and observe about the Moon is that, just like the Sun, it rises in the east and sets in the west each day. All celestial bodies do this, because the Earth is turning on its axis (at a speed of about 1000 mph or 1600 km/hr near the equator, no less).

However, to complicate matters somewhat, the moon also migrates across the sky's dome each day due to its own orbit around the Earth. This is a slower, less obviously visible motion and can best be marked against the fixed stars over a period of hours.

The Moon takes about one month to orbit the Earth, so with each day that means it will move between 12 and 13 degrees in relation to any fixed stars.

Since what you will see when you look up at the night sky depends on the time of year, it is worth collecting relevant charts. These can be freely and easily downloaded from the internet.

The example below is taken from the time of writing, in winter.

Winter Astronomy Highlights

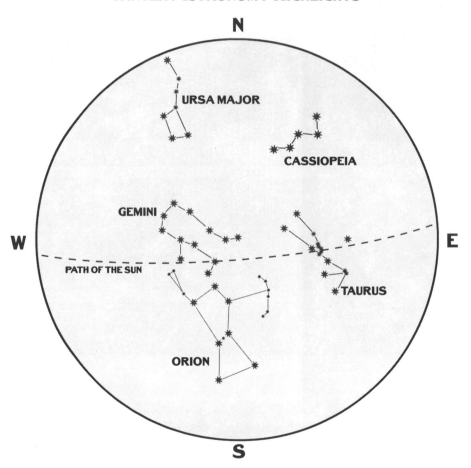

Charts like this are aimed at beginners but as your skills as a stargazer improve you may want to invest in a printed chart as well as a planisphere, which is a star chart made up of two adjustable discs that can be rotated to display the visible stars for any time and date.

Don't rush out to buy a telescope just yet, you can do plenty of stargazing to begin with using a decent pair of binoculars. Point them at any bright objects you see in the sky (but not directly at the Sun). If you are far enough away from the city and light pollution you might even find hazy patches in the sky: these are star clusters made up of clouds of gas and dust where new stars are forming.

If it's summer and the sky is dark enough, look for the starlit band that is the Milky Way.

To be a true stargazer, you will need to learn constellations. The best way to do this is by noticing patterns among the stars. Like learning the streets on a map, once you can connect one pattern with another one nearby, you can expand your field of knowledge to take in a wider and wider area of sky.

It is exciting to think, as you do this, that as long as humankind has been around, people have been doing exactly what you are doing now. By looking at the stars, our ancestors tried to make meaning of the universe, just as you are doing.

This is a process that takes time – you simply can't learn the night sky all at once – but it provides an inexhaustible thrill and a journey of discovery that will reward a lifetime's worth of curiosity.

KUBB

'We don't stop playing because we get old; we get old
because we stop playing ' **VICTOR HUGO**

W hen they weren't sailing around Europe looking to pillage and mur-
der, the Vikings, like all of us, needed some down time. The popular
game of Kubb (rhymes with 'tube') was thought to be one of their favourite
hobbies.

Kubb is similar to skittles and even shares some ancestry with ten-pin bowling. The objective is to use wooden batons to knock over the 'kubbs' (heavier,
rectangular blocks of wood) on the opposing side of the pitch before your
opponent does. The fact it can be played on almost any surface – grass, ice,
sand, concrete, you name it – and the relative simplicity of crafting the playing
pieces yourself, makes it fun and worthwhile. It can also be fiercely addictive.

HOW TO PLAY

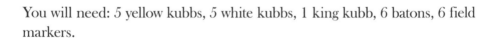

You will need: 5 yellow kubbs, 5 white kubbs, 1 king kubb, 6 batons, 6 field
markers.

Kubb can be played by 2–12 players and, as an added bonus, uneven teams
don't offer an advantage to either side (so you won't need to pester any nearby
friends who might be enjoying lying down with a glass of wine). The game can
take anything from 20 minutes to several hours to play.

The goal is to be the first team to knock down all your kubbs and then the
'king'. Knocking down the king without knocking down the kubbs is like pot-
ting the black ball in snooker out of turn and will instantly lose you the game.

First, set out a 16x26 foot field, using rocks, stakes (or beer bottles) in the corners. Place the king in the centre and evenly spread five kubbs along each baseline.

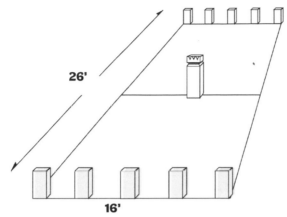

26'

16'

1. The first (white) team throw their batons at the kubbs on the opposite baseline.

Batons must be thrown underhand and must travel straight or end over end. They cannot be thrown horizontally or sidearm.

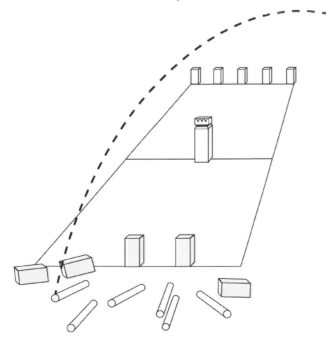

2. Once the first team have thrown their batons, the second (yellow) team stand at their baseline and throw any kubbs that have been knocked over back into the other half of the field. These are then known as 'field kubbs'. The yellow team has two chances to throw each kubb into the opposite half of the field. If they throw the kubb out of bounds twice in a row, the offending kubb is placed 6 inches behind the king.

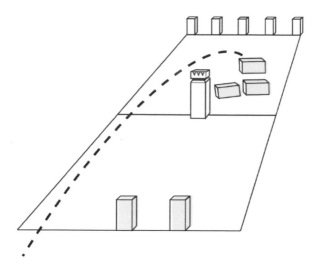

3. Once all the field kubbs have been thrown, the white team stands them up on end. If a kubb was thrown and it hit another field kubb, then those kubbs are stacked on top of each other. (There is no limit to the number of kubbs that can be stacked in this way.)

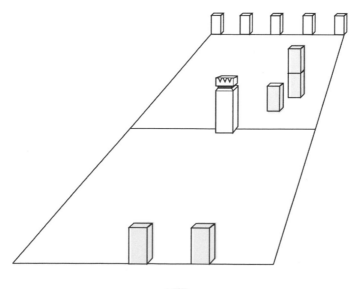

4. The yellow team must then knock down all the field kubbs before they may throw at the baseline kubbs. Any baseline kubbs that get knocked down before the field kubbs do not count and must be stood back up.

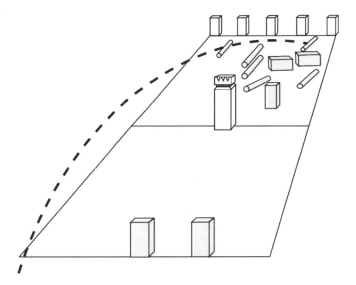

5. Once the yellow team have finished throwing, the white team pick up any knocked-down kubbs (both 'field' and on the baseline) and throw them back into the opposite half of the field for the first team to stand up.

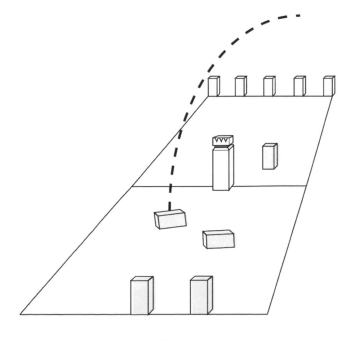

6. If the yellow team left any field kubbs standing, then the white team may throw their batons from behind an imaginary line, which runs parallel to the kubb closest to the king.

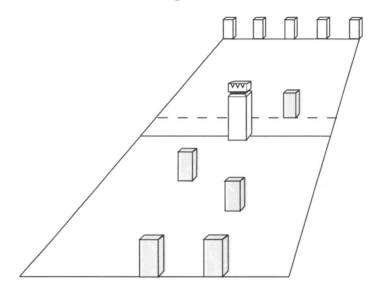

Play continues in this way until either team knocks over all the opposing field and baseline kubbs. Once they have done this they must then attempt to knock down the king kubb. All attempts on the king must be taken from the baseline. Once the king is knocked down, the game is over.

CRAFTING THE KUBB SET

A KUBB SET CONSISTS OF THE FOLLOWING:

- Ten kubbs – rectangular wooden blocks 15 cm tall and 7 cm square on the end.
- One king, a larger wooden piece 30 cm tall and 9 cm square on the end, sometimes adorned with a crown design on the top
- Six batons, 30 cm long and 4.4 cm in diameter.
- Six field marking pins, four to designate the corners of the pitch, and two to mark the centreline

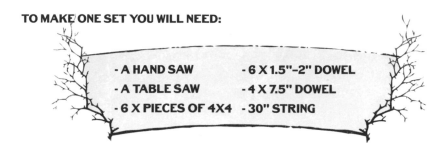

- A HAND SAW   - 6 X 1.5"–2" DOWEL
- A TABLE SAW   - 4 X 7.5" DOWEL
- 6 X PIECES OF 4X4   - 30" STRING

The first step is to make the 'king kubb'. Using the hand saw, chop 12" from the 4x4. How much you decorate the king (if you choose to decorate it at all) is up to you and will depend on your woodwork skills. We used a table saw to make two 45-degree cuts to notch the sides and a series of cuts to decorate the top (as pictured). You could just as well use paints or even a marker pen to personalise your kings.

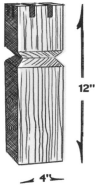

12"

4"

The next step is to trim the rest of the wood.

The other pieces, the kubbs, are narrower than the king piece, so you will need a table saw to cut them to size. The dimensions are 7 cm x 7 cm x 15 cm (or 2.75" x 2.75" x 6"). So, trim .75" from the two sides of the 4x4. Now that the wood is at the right size, simply chop 10 x 6" lengths to create your ten pieces.

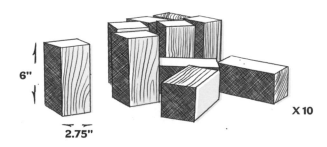

6"

2.75"

X 10

Next, you need to create the six batons. These should be chopped from the 1.5–2" dowels at roughly 12" long. You can also create an extra four, to be used as stakes to mark out the field, by cutting the same length from the 0.75" dowels.

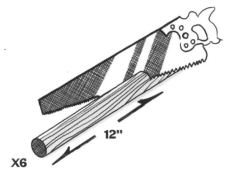

'THE SEA, ONCE IT CASTS ITS
SPELL, HOLDS ONE IN ITS NET
OF WONDER FOREVER'
JACQUES COUSTEAU

REAL-WORLD TREASURES

'Everyone on earth has a treasure that awaits him'

PAULO COELHO

What greater adventure is there than to head out into the wild, pickaxe and map in hand, in search of hidden treasure? The prospect of gold, gems, and priceless artefacts waiting to be discovered has captured the imagination of treasure-hunters for centuries. It is the stuff of fantasy. Unlikely as it may seem, though, there are real-life undiscovered treasures still out there, just waiting for explorers with the right amount of gumption (and a good deal of luck) to find them.

Here are five real-world treasures yet to be discovered...

BUTCH CASSIDY'S HIDDEN TREASURE

Arguably the most famous outlaw of them all, Robert Leroy Parker, or 'Butch Cassidy' as he would come to be known, was the first of 13 children born to British immigrant parents in 1866. Growing up in the town of Beaver, Utah, Parker was drawn into petty crime at a young age before he went on to become the leader of the infamous Wild Bunch gang that terrorised the American Old West at the end of the 19th-century. Cassidy and his gang were responsible for a staggering number of daring and deadly robberies of trains and banks that netted them hundreds of thousands of dollars in loot.

Cassidy famously paired up with Harry Alonzo Longabaugh (better known to us all as 'the Sundance Kid').

Pursued for years by the Pinkerton detective agency, the pair were ultimately forced to flee the United States, first to Argentina and then finally to Bolivia, where they were killed in a shootout in 1908, after trying to rob a silver mine.

Some believe, though, that before he fled the US for the last time, Cassidy buried a stash of loot somewhere in Irish Canyon, in the northwestern part of Colorado, Moffat County. This remote valley was a favoured retreat of Cassidy and his Wild Bunch when the law were hot on their tail. The stash is believed to be $20,000 in cash.

THE FORREST FENN TREASURES

Forrest Fenn is a millionaire art collector who, after being diagnosed with terminal cancer in 1988, decided to hide a treasure chest filled with his most valuable possessions as his legacy. Believed to be worth between one and three million dollars, the treasure is made up of gold nuggets, rare coins, jewellery and gemstones, as well as a copy of Fenn's autobiography (though we are guessing not too many people are on the hunt because of that).

Against the odds, though, Fenn survived the cancer and in 2010, when he reached the ripe age of 80, he decided to bury the treasure anyway and watch as people scrambled to find it. Fenn has hidden his bounty somewhere in the Rocky Mountains and left the necessary clues within the pages of his autobiography (which might lead you to conclude if nothing else that Fenn is good at marketing). Fenn himself also periodically gives out clues – the most recent of which came in January 2015 when he stated: 'I know the treasure chest is wet.'

As whimsical as all this might sound, several treasure hunters have gone missing in search of Fenn's elusive bounty – the most recent of whom was found dead in July 2016!

SALZBURG   VIENNA

NAZI TREASURES IN LAKE TOPLITZ

Lake Toplitz is hidden away at the base of a dense mountain forest within the Austrian Alps. As if the place weren't creepy enough, the lake is so deep that at its bottom there is not one molecule of oxygen in the water: it is quite literally lifeless.

The Nazis originally used the lake's shore as a naval testing station during the Second World War. However, as the tide of the war turned against them and defeat became inevitable, they began to use the lake to dispose of ill-gotten and blood-stained treasures they had stolen.

Some treasure has already been recovered from the site, including millions in fake currency, which the Nazis had intended to use in a devastating attack on the Allies' economies (known as Operation Bernhard).

However, many believe that they also sank millions of dollars' worth of gold and diamonds, as well as priceless works of art, that have yet to be found. This theory is given credence by an artfully sunken layer of logs which reduces visibility and also makes diving near impossible. Indeed, divers have lost their lives while trying to reach the lake's bottom and uncover the mystery.

THE TREASURE OF LIMA

After the Spanish conquest of Peru in the 16th-century, the country remained under Spanish control for centuries. The Spanish empire had accumulated vast wealth from its plunder of the New World, and Peru's capital, Lima, became the holding place for this unimaginably grand treasure.

However, in 1820 the Peruvians revolted and forced the Spanish into a hasty evacuation. Having to think quickly, the Viceroy of Lima chose to transport some of the loot to Mexico and entrusted the commander of a British merchant ship, the *Mary Dear*, with the task of transporting what is estimated to have been between a $12 million and $60 million fortune.

Captain William Thompson and his crew, though, proved unable to resist the temptation and turned pirate, slitting the throats of their Spanish guards as well as the accompanying priests before throwing them overboard.

The pirates then headed for the nearby Cocos Island, off the coast of what is now Costa Rica, where they buried the treasure. Though the *Mary Dear* was subsequently captured, Thompson and his first mate survived by promising to lead the Spanish to their treasure in return for their lives (though the rest of the crew were hanged for their crimes).

Once they reached the Cocos Islands, however, the pair escaped into the jungle and vanished along with the treasure, which remains undiscovered to this day.

THE FLOR DO MAR

The *Flor do Mar*, which translates as 'Flower of the Sea', was a 16th-century Portuguese carrack (the largest sailing ship of its day) built to ferry the empire's riches back from the Indies.

The *Flor do Mar*'s longevity was remarkable. At a time when Indian ships were built for three or four years' service at most, the ship's almost ten years of duty was a marvel. However, the ship had long been known to be unseaworthy and it was misplaced pride as much as anything that kept her in service. As so often, this hubris would come at a price.

On what would become the ship's final voyage, King Alfonso had tasked her with bringing home the vast fortune received as a tribute from the King of Siam. She was caught in a storm in the strait of Malacca (a stretch of water between what is now the Malay peninsula and the island of Sumatra) and wrecked on shoals, sinking to rest on the seabed deep beneath the waves.

To this day, no one knows exactly where the *Flor do Mar* lies, and there is some controversy over which country controls the area and salvage rights where she is thought to have vanished.

Whoever finds this treasure, however, will discover over sixty tons of gold as well as diamonds said to be the size of a man's fist.

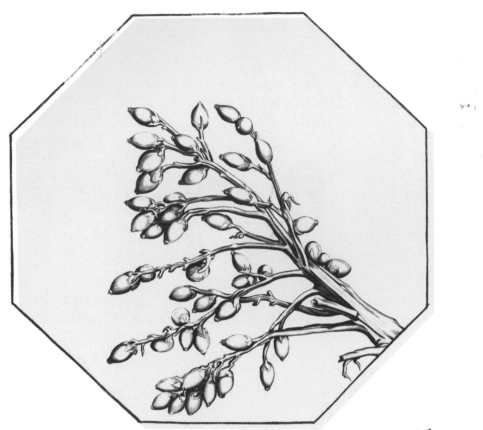

'**AT SOME POINT
IN LIFE, THE WORLD'S
BEAUTY BECOMES
ENOUGH**'

TONI MORRISON

OUTDOOR PIZZA OVEN

'Unless you are a pizza, the answer is yes, I can live without you'

BILL MURRAY

Pizza can be delicious in its many different forms. Only a snob would deny that a piping-hot slice of extra-cheesy, extra-doughy goodness from your local takeaway can be just what's wanted (particularly after a few pints of an evening). However, for those in the know, there is only one way to make true, Neapolitan-style pizza and that is using a brick oven. The difference is apparent after the first bite, and more so when the whole thing is made and enjoyed with friends sitting out under the stars.

The burning wood used in a real oven provides an incredibly strong source of heat (at its hottest, a brick oven will reach anywhere between 570 and 660 degrees Fahrenheit), which radiates across the dome while the floor of the oven remains cooler, meaning that, as opposed to your late-night special from the high street, your pizza won't go soggy and its crust will reach a state of delicious crispness. Similarly, your chosen toppings will be cooked in a flash, with all their moisture and flavour kept locked in.

This is not an easy undertaking and will require real planning, patience and persistence, but we found the process incredibly rewarding. And, as if the promise of year-round pizza weren't enough, with a wood-fired pizza oven in your backyard, you'll be able to bake more than just pizza.

Needless to say, when using a pizza oven special care must be taken as the inside surface will reach incredibly high temperatures.

There are several ways to build a pizza oven and a variety of materials that you can use, including clay, brick, adobe and concrete. The important thing is to use a material that holds in heat. We have chosen to make our oven using the simplest technique: bricks, sand and cement.

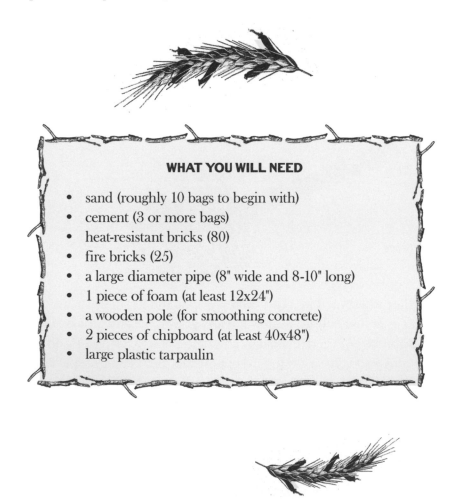

WHAT YOU WILL NEED

- sand (roughly 10 bags to begin with)
- cement (3 or more bags)
- heat-resistant bricks (80)
- fire bricks (25)
- a large diameter pipe (8" wide and 8-10" long)
- 1 piece of foam (at least 12x24")
- a wooden pole (for smoothing concrete)
- 2 pieces of chipboard (at least 40x48")
- large plastic tarpaulin

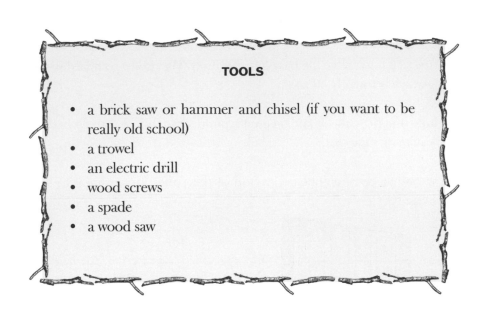

TOOLS

- a brick saw or hammer and chisel (if you want to be really old school)
- a trowel
- an electric drill
- wood screws
- a spade
- a wood saw

WHERE TO BUILD

When choosing the location for your oven, there are three important things to bear in mind. First, the height and the weight: even the smallest ovens are incredibly heavy.

Next, you will need a strong base. We chose to make ours using a wooden pallet, as this is the simplest and quickest way, but if your oven is to be a permanent fixture then you should consider building a cement base. Not only will this look better but it will also raise the oven to a height that is easier to use.

The third thing to consider is the heat: the oven will reach very high temperatures, so before you begin your build, consider the surrounding space. Be careful to find somewhere without any fire hazards and where your oven won't cause smoke damage.

THE BUILD

The first step is to create the base for your oven. We used a standard wooden pallet, which is roughly 40"x48".

1. Make sure the pallet is laid on even ground, or on top of your cement base if you're making one.

2. Lay one piece of chipboard on top of the pallet (trimming it to size if necessary).

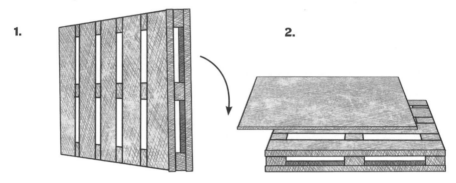

3. Use the wood saw to cut pieces from the other piece of chipboard (at least 4" in width) to form a perimeter around the base of the chip board. These will hold the cement that you are going to pour to create the base.

4. Once the perimeter has been nailed together and secured to the wooden pallet, pour in a thick layer of concrete (between 3 and 4 inches) and smooth it out with the baton. The concrete base will take several days to dry, during which time you may be tempted to call your local pizza delivery place. Don't.

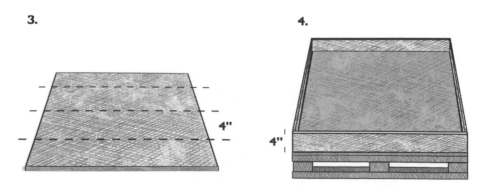

Once the base has dried, the next step is to lay the base of your oven design. Typically, you want an arched opening that leads to a half-dome oven. We chopped our bricks in half, as that gave us more flexibility in the design.

Lay the base outline of bricks, leaving a gap at the front which will form the front arch to the oven.

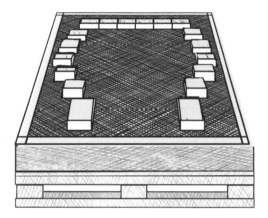

Once your outline is in place, you will need to form the arch of the oven. Be sure to leave an opening that is wide enough for you to work the fire and to easily reach the pizzas.

Use long, uncut bricks to create the base of the arch.

Take the piece of foam and cut it to form the shape of a bridge. This will temporarily support the bricks forming the arch. (Bear in mind that the arch will end up being roughly ⅔ the height of the overall oven.)

The next step is to cement the bricks. A good trick is to use sand to support the shape of the oven as you give the cement time to dry.

1. Cement the base outline of bricks together, before laying the large plastic sheet over them.

2. Pack sand on top of the sheet along the inside edge of the brick outline. This will help to hold them in place. (The plastic sheet is there to stop the wet cement mixing with the sand)

1.
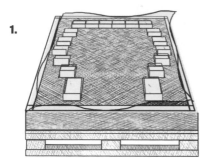

2.
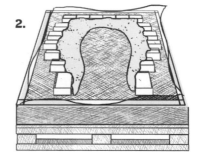

3. Once the cement has dried, add sand and layers of brick, and continue to do so until your brickwork has reached a height several inches above the arch (and the belly of tightly packed sand).

Cement the arch bricks in place.

Leave a hole for your chimney between the arch and the dome and then insert the chimney (made from the pipe), making sure it sits higher than the opening of the archway, so the smoke will exit via the chimney.

3.

SPACE FOR CHIMNEY

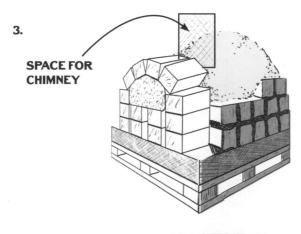

Now it's time to create the concrete outer layer. This will not only smooth the outside of your oven but will also add a crucial layer of insulation to help your oven reach blisteringly high temperatures.

Coat the outside surface of the oven with a generous amount of concrete and smooth it over using the trowel.

Once the outer layer dries after a couple of days, remove the support structure of the foam, sand and plastic sheet.

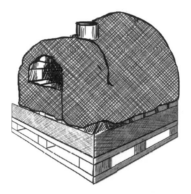

It's cooking time! Once the concrete has dried, you can light the first fire. This will serve to check whether your oven is indeed fully dry and ready to use. So long as no cracks appear where smoke is escaping, then the structure is sound.

Simply put, a good pizza fire involves lots of kindling and a good deal of attention paid to create the optimum heat source. Since much has been written (and, we imagine, many a Neapolitan vendetta begun) on the subject, we would encourage you to do a bit of further research as well as your own experimentation in the quest for the perfect cooking conditions.

KITES

'Throw your dreams into space like a kite, and you do not know what it will bring back, a new life, a new friend, a new love, a new country.'

ANAIS NIN

To fly a kite conjures the image of an afternoon of Mary Poppins-esque pleasure in the park. Kites, though, have a long and colourful history that goes far beyond the playground. Invented in China in the 5th century BC, where the silk and bamboo needed to make them were in rich supply, the first kites were used for serious business such as measuring distances, passing military signals, and even transporting men and materials.

The Europeans and their American cousins were relatively late to the party, and it wasn't until the 18th century that scientists began to catch on to the technological breakthroughs kite-flying could offer.

Many of us know the tale (quite possibly not true, by the way) of Benjamin Franklin flying a kite to prove that lightning was caused by electricity, but kites were also instrumental to the Wright Brothers' research as they sought to achieve the first manned flight in the late 1800s.

And that is because the physics that draws a kite up into the air is also at work to keep a 900,000 lb Boeing 747 at 40,000 feet. The 'lift' that makes a kite fly happens when the air flowing around its surface produces low pressure above and high pressure below the wings, thus drawing it upward – just as with your long-haul flight to New York.

Even knowing, as we do, the science that causes the kite to stay in the air, the effect is no less magic for it. And Mary Poppins was surely right that when we hold a kite up in the perfect blue sky it sends our heart soaring too...

HOW TO BUILD A KITE

There are countless designs you can follow, each with subtly different properties, but we chose what we feel is the classic and the simplest to build: the diamond.

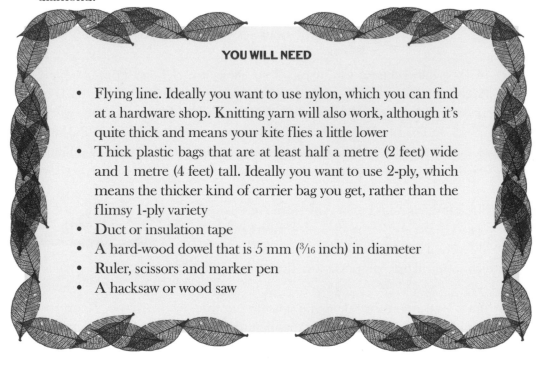

YOU WILL NEED

- Flying line. Ideally you want to use nylon, which you can find at a hardware shop. Knitting yarn will also work, although it's quite thick and means your kite flies a little lower
- Thick plastic bags that are at least half a metre (2 feet) wide and 1 metre (4 feet) tall. Ideally you want to use 2-ply, which means the thicker kind of carrier bag you get, rather than the flimsy 1-ply variety
- Duct or insulation tape
- A hard-wood dowel that is 5 mm (3/16 inch) in diameter
- Ruler, scissors and marker pen
- A hacksaw or wood saw

STEP 1

First, you need to measure out your sail:

Lie the plastic bag out on the floor, with the open end at the bottom. Beginning just below the bag's top-left corner, measure with your eye 3 dots on the plastic (as shown in the illustration) and mark them with the marker pen.

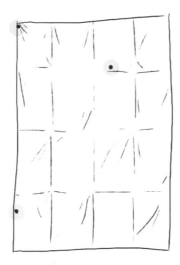

STEP 2

Next, you need to cut out the sail:

Connect the dots using the ruler and pen before flipping over the plastic bag and tracing all the black lines.

Now use the scissors to cut along the top and right-hand side of the bag, and open it out to reveal the outline of your sail.

Use the scissors to cut along all the lines.

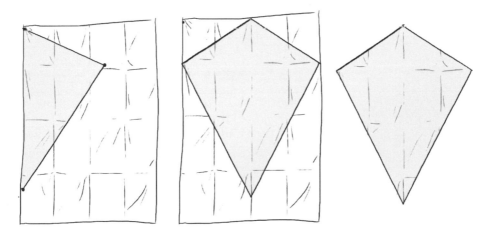

STEP 3

Add the spars:

Place a length of dowel down the sail's centre line, lining it up with the top sail corner before sawing it off at the bottom corner.

Cut a small strip of insulation tape, roughly 5cm, and fix the dowel to the bag. Repeat this with the bottom end of the dowel. Do the same for the other dowel.

STEP 4

To attach the flying line:
At the point where the dowels cross, pierce a hole in the sail and thread the free end of your flying line through this hole before tying it around the crossing-point of the dowels.

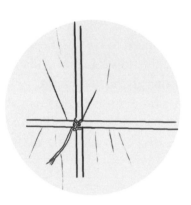

STEP 5

Finally you need to fix the tail to your kite:
Using off-cuts of the plastic bag and the scissors, make long strips, roughly five times as long as the kite and about 5 cm wide.
Tie one of the tail's ends around the base of the vertical spar and then use a knot to tie the tail to the dowel.

FLYING THE KITE

To get the most out of your kite, you want at least a medium-strength wind. Alternately pull in and let out the line to make your kite move around in the sky.

Always fly your kite in open spaces, away from power lines, buildings, drones, planes and anything else that might present a hazard.

Buildings and trees can also cause air turbulence that can draw your kite in.

Navigate Using the Stars

'I have loved the stars too fondly to be fearful of the night'

GALILEO

In an age when satellite navigation is often at our fingertips, few of us are likely to ever need to find our way using one of the oldest methods known to mankind. However, as with so many of the 'old ways', there is a special kind of thrill that comes from doing things yourself and studies have even shown that developing navigational skills can enhance your intelligence. So, at the very least, by learning to navigate you will be able to feel superior to your friends.

There are endlessly sophisticated methods of finding your way using the night sky. However, to start with, you can find north, south, east and west simply by learning a few stars and constellations, or you can pick out a star and follow its movements.

METHOD 1: LOOK FOR POLARIS, THE NORTH STAR
Polaris is the brightest star in the constellation Ursa Minor, or the Little Bear. The constellation was so named by the ancient Greeks who, rather strangely, thought that bears had long tails. Polaris is found in the bear's 'tail'.

Today, Ursa Minor is more commonly known as the Little Dipper, rather than Little Bear. This is because its seven stars are thought to look more like a small water dipper.

Even so, you will find that most of the names given to the constellations require more than a little interpretive imagination.

Although Polaris is visible in the northern sky from most places north of the equator, it can be difficult to find if you don't know quite what you're researching for. To help, you can use stars from other constellations to lead the way to Polaris.

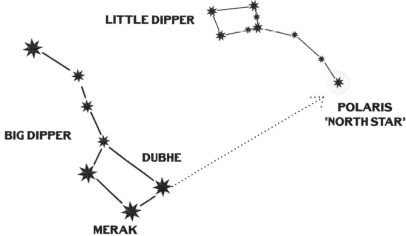

The most common, and simplest, pointer stars are Dubhe and Merak, the two stars on the edge of the Big Dipper opposite its handle. If you follow these stars in the direction of the mouth of the Big Dipper, you will find Polaris.

When the Big Dipper is below the horizon – during the early hours in autumn, for instance – you can draw a line through the stars on the eastern edge formed by the Great Square of Pegasus, Algenib and Alpheratz (part of the constellation Andromeda), and through Caph, the star at the far right edge of the constellation Cassiopeia.

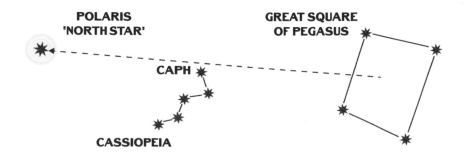

METHOD 2: FIND YOUR LATITUDE

(Note: these methods apply to the northern hemisphere only.)

First, you must locate Polaris, using the previous method. Once you have Polaris, you need to work out the angle in degrees between Polaris's position and the northern horizon. The best and most accurate way to do this is with a quadrant or sextant. If you're not an 18th-century seaman and don't have one of these to hand, worry not: you can approximate the angle by extending your fist to the horizon and stacking fists one on top of the other until you reach the North Star – each extended fist represents roughly 10 degrees of angle measure.

METHOD 3: FIND SOUTH

In this case, you will need to locate Orion, the Hunter (again use your imagination liberally). In reality, it looks more like a bent hourglass. The stars Bellatrix and Betelgeuse represent its shoulders, while the stars Saiph and Rigel are its knees or feet. The three stars in the middle, Alnitak, Alnilam and Mintaka, make up Orion's belt. (In the northern hemisphere, Orion can be seen mainly during the winter and early spring, though it can be seen late at night in the autumn or before sunrise in the summer.)

First, you must find Orion's sword. This looks like one fairly bright star, one dim and one fuzzy-looking star hanging from Alnilam, the middle star on Orion's belt. This 'sword' points south. Interestingly, that slightly strange-looking 'fuzzy' star is in fact the Great Nebula of Orion: a miraculous inter-stellar cradle where new stars are born.

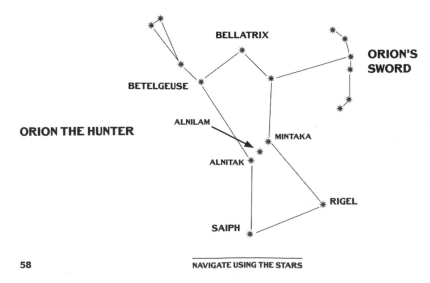

BELLATRIX

ORION'S SWORD

BETELGEUSE

ORION THE HUNTER

ALNILAM

MINTAKA

ALNITAK

RIGEL

SAIPH

METHOD 4: FINDING SOUTH IN THE SOUTHERN HEMISPHERE

To do this, you will need to locate Crux, the Southern Cross, which is made up of four stars that form the ends of the cross's upright and crosspiece. (The Southern Cross so dominates the night sky that it is featured on the flags of Australia and New Zealand.)

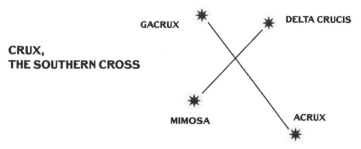

CRUX, THE SOUTHERN CROSS

GACRUX
DELTA CRUCIS
MIMOSA
ACRUX

Now that you have located Crux, you must extend a line through the long axis of its cross. The point along this line roughly four and a half times the length of the long axis is directly above south.

Admittedly that's not the most accurate of methods and if you're searching for a well in the middle of the desert then that margin could mean life or death. So, to improve your accuracy, you can find two 'pointers' to the Southern Cross and draw a line through them. Then, draw a line perpendicular from the middle of that and extend it to intersect with the line you have drawn from the Southern Cross. The point at which they intersect is directly above south.

METHOD 5: FINDING EAST OR WEST (CELESTIAL EQUATOR)

First, look for the constellation Orion, as above. You need to locate the star furthest to the right in Orion's belt, Mintaka. This star rises and sets within one degree of true east or west.

METHOD 6: FINDING A DIRECTION BY FOLLOWING A STAR'S POSITION (ANY- WHERE)

First you will need to drive two stakes into the ground. Ideally, these should be roughly the size of cricket stumps, but really you can work with anything, though you may need to crouch. The stakes should be placed roughly one yard apart. Pick a star, any star, from the night sky. In practice, the brighter the better, as you don't want to risk losing sight of it. Then line the star up with the tops of both stakes (as pictured on the next page).

Now wait for the star to move out of position with the stakes. The Earth's rotation, from west to east, causes the stars as a whole to rotate from east to west. So, which way the star has moved in relation to its original position will allow you to work out which direction you are facing.

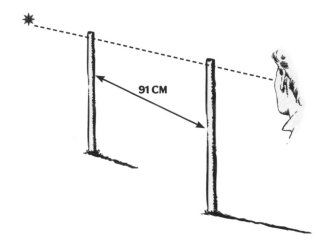

91 CM

WATER WHEEL

'The water wheel accepts water and turns and gives it away, weeping'

RUMI

Water wheels have been in existence almost as long as humans have been using other things to do their work for them. In fact, they were still widespread throughout the West during much of the last century: milling flour, grinding wood or even hammering wrought iron, before being overtaken by other (noisier, messier and more polluting) technologies.

Water wheels remain, though, one of the most environmentally friendly and sustainable methods of creating energy. And, as we built our small-scale version, we found great pleasure in creating such an ingeniously simple machine to draw power from the natural world.

There are two fundamental systems of water wheels: horizontal and vertical. We have chosen to build a vertical system, for its uncanny ability seemingly to defy gravity.

WHAT YOU WILL NEED

- scissors
- 2 large cardboard sheets
- a pen
- a protractor
- a wood or plastic skewer

Use the scissors to cut a long piece from one side of the cardboard, 3 inches wide by 18 inches long (7.5 x 45 cm).

Using the pen and then the scissors, cut the piece into ten 2-inch (5 cm) sections. These sections are going to form your paddles.

2"

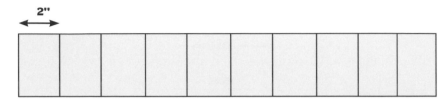

X10

Using the protractor and pen, mark out two 7-inch (17.5 cm) circles on the cardboard.

The protractor will help you to draw an even circle, and will also show you where the centre of the circle will be. Your axle, made from the skewer, is going to go through the centre, connecting the two sides of the wheel and allowing it to spin.

6"

Use the pen to draw an outline of the wheel's stand by tracing an 'A' shape on the cardboard. The 'A' should be 5 inches tall and 5 inches wide (12.5 cm x 12.5 cm). Mark a small 'v' at the top middle point of the 'A'. The axle is going to slot into this groove.

To make the water wheel stand's supports, mark out two 3-inch long and 1-inch wide rectangles (7.5 cm x 2.5 cm).

Use the scissors to cut out the outlines you drew for the wheel's sides as well as the stand and the supports.

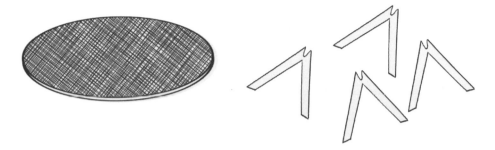

Place the side of the wheel flat on the floor and use the protractor to measure out and mark the positions for the paddles. Each paddle needs to be set at a 45-degree angle to the next paddle and at a diagonal towards the wheel's centre point.

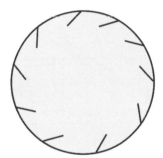

Use the glue to stick the side of the paddles to the water wheel, according to the marks that you have made with your pen. Repeat for the other side of the wheel.

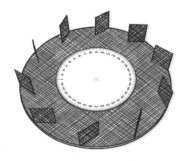

Pierce the skewer through the centre point of the wheels, so it goes through both sides and is sticking out the same amount on each.

Next, use the glue to stick the A- frame to the support plates you made earlier. Begin with the right-hand side of the frame, taking care to place the 'leg' centrally on the plate. Repeat for the left-hand side.

Rest the wooden skewer on the axle by slotting it into the v-shaped insets that you created earlier. The wheel is now in its stand.

Once this is done, repeat with the other A- frame.

Rest the wooden skewer on the axle by slotting it into the v-shaped notches that you made earlier.

To test that the wheel is spinning freely, start carefully by putting it in some running water that isn't too vigorous, e.g. a gently flowing stream.

If that goes **OK** and everything is turning as it should, then you can test how much weight your wheel can handle by tying some string to the wheel's axle and at the other end of the string attaching a cup, so that when the wheel turns it pulls the cup with it.

SLOE GIN

'The gin and tonic has saved more Englishmen's lives,
and minds, than all the doctors in the empire'
WINSTON CHURCHILL

To be in the presence of nature can be an intoxicating experience, and that's never so true as when you allow nature to ferment a little before quaffing it down.

Of course, you can always go and buy your tipple of choice from the local shop, but there is so much more fun to be had spending a day out in the wild, fighting brambles and slogging through mud, before coming home to make and enjoy your own hard-earned liquor.

Sloe gin gets its beautiful ruby colour from the sloe drupes (a relative of the plum) found on blackthorn trees. Ripe sloes are traditionally picked after the first winter frost, which occurs from late October to early November in the northern hemisphere.

Blackthorn trees are usually found in scrub, copses and woodlands, and since they are commonly used as a hedging plant they can be prickly, unforgiving customers – so pick carefully.

You can search for sloes on foot or, if you know a good river spot, then searching for them by canoe can be good fun.

Blackthorn trees are spindly and thorny, as their name suggests, and the fruit they bear, though it looks seductive with its blue-black colouring and yellow flesh, is especially bitter. Don't worry, they taste better in the bottle.

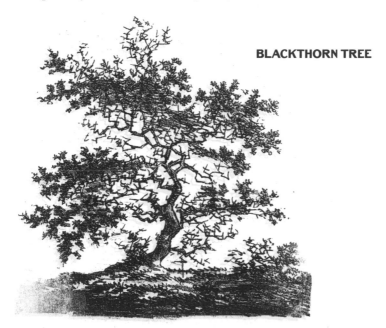

BLACKTHORN TREE

When it comes to the gin-making process, as the old adage goes, 'Good things come to those who...' and in the case of sloe gin, it's a good long six months' fermentation. While sloe gin will taste fine from three months onwards, it's worth persevering for the fullest flavour that comes with time.

INGREDIENTS

1 LITRE/1¾ PINT GIN
(THE BETTER THE
QUALITY, THE BETTER THE
DRINK WILL TASTE)

450G/1LB SLOES

225G/8OZ CASTER
SUGAR

METHOD

1. You want to prick through the tough skin of the sloes with a sterilised needle to allow the berries to release their flavour into the gin. (One particular folk tale says that one should not prick the sloes with a metal fork unless it is made of silver.)

    However, if that sounds like too much work, you can put them in the freezer overnight instead. As the berries freeze, their skin will burst, giving the same result.

2. Place the sloes in a large jar or bottle.

3. Add the sugar and gin and seal tightly before shaking vigorously for a good few minutes.

4. The gin and sloe mixture must be stored in a cool, dark place and shaken every two days during the first week. After that, shake it once a week for up to six months. (The sugar should have completely dissolved before the end of the first week.)

5. Finally, after three to six months are up, remove the sloes and any leftover bits by straining your gin through a piece of cloth or muslin.

BIRD CALLING

'A bird does not sing because it has an answer.
It sings because it has a song' **JOAN WALSH ANGLUND**

Like humans, birds are talkative creatures. Indeed, just about every species of bird produces some kind of vocal sound (only storks, pelicans and vultures are resolutely silent) using either 'calls' – a brief sound made up of a simple acoustic structure, such as a squawk, a cheep, or a chatter, etc. – or 'songs', which are relatively long series of notes, often taking the form of a melody.

Different calls and songs serve a variety of purposes, all of which unsurprisingly relate to reproduction in some way. For this reason, the majority of calling is done by males and will be variously to do with establishing territory, finding mates and beginning courtship.

The patterns of song and call are endlessly complex and so the skill of bird-calling that we are practising here is simply about creating an interesting sound that will carry through the woods. When done correctly, you will discover it is stunningly loud. We are not attempting to trick a bird into courting with you... This is not that kind of book.

USING YOUR HANDS TO MAKE A BIRD-CALLING SOUND
STEP 1: Get your hands into position. (This shouldn't matter whether you are left- or right-handed, but if it feels uncomfortable then try switching round.)

First, place the left edge of your right hand with palm up at the base of your fingers of your left hand.

Pivot your right hand on its left edge so that your palms are facing each other.

Curl the fingertips of both hands around, so that your hands are clamped together.

Your right-hand thumb will be lower than the thumb of your left hand. Without moving your hands from this position, move your left-hand thumb upward, so that both thumbs are aligned.

Your hands are now in the position they need to be to do the call.

STEP 2: THE BLOWING TECHNIQUE

First, pucker your lips. (Do this away from your hands. You will draw your hands to your lips once you're ready to exhale.)

To inhale properly you must draw as much air as possible into your throat, rather than your chest. Ignore everything that your drama teacher might have taught you, and breathe in so that your shoulders draw up.

Hold that breath behind your puckered lips.

Next, bring your hands to your lips. You should place your lips over your knuckles.

Keep your hands locked tightly. If they are loose, then air will escape out of the sides. At the same time, you need a little space between them to allow the air to flow.

Blow hard and keep your hands steady.

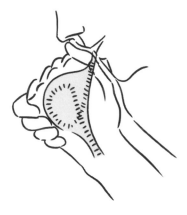

STEP 3 CALLING LIKE A BOSS
Once you have produced a decent sound (and it may take some practice to get there), you may want to try altering the pitch of the note by moving your hands. After some practice, you can get to the point where you are able to produce a melody.

- Bringing your hands closer together will produce a higher pitch
- Pulling them further apart will produce a lower pitch

After some practice, we were able to create a not-unpleasant sound (that might generously be called a melody) that carried right through the wood.

BIRD WATCHING

'In order to see birds, it is necessary to become part of the silence.
One has to sit still like a mystic and wait'

ROBERT LYND

As with so many things that might once have been thought of as painfully uncool and, let's be honest, downright nerdy, bird watching – or 'birding' – is enjoying something of a renaissance. And with good reason.

Once you put images of anoraks from your mind, you begin to appreciate that birding provides an amazing opportunity to venture out into the world, to look and listen, in a way that is uniquely relaxing and enriching. We don't know whether therapists recommend bird-watching but, from our experience, they should.

Beyond the joy of it, the other great thing to recommend bird watching is its simplicity and accessibility. Just about anyone, anywhere can get involved, with nothing more than a pair of binoculars, a field guide and a yearning to discover.

Birding is about observation and the object is to study the birds in their natural environment to draw yourself closer to them and their world.

For that reason, it is important to be respectful and not to harm the birds nor damage their environment in any way.

This means do not stress the birds with artificial lighting or recording equipment (camera flashes, etc.).

Do not get too close to nests or feeding sites, so as not to interfere with the birds' activities. And don't attract birds to areas where they might be in danger from dogs or cats.

PREPARING EQUIPMENT

First you will need a pair of binoculars with decent magnification (something from 7x or 8x ideally), but which aren't too heavy. The rule of thumb is that light-weight is better for cluttered environments such as woodlands or forest, while heavier pairs suit open country and wetlands.

You will naturally choose a pair of binoculars according to how much you want to spend (or which ever pair you might happen to have lying around at home) but an important thing to bear in mind is the strap: since this weight is going to be hanging round your neck for hours at a time, you will need to be comfortable.

Before you set off, you need to calibrate your binoculars according to the manufacturer's instructions.

Next, you will need your field guide. Some people prefer illustrations to photographs, since they arguably give a truer representation of plumage and colours, etc. We have illustrated a few of the birds that we spotted, but you will need a guide that is relevant to your local area.

Before you set out, it is a good idea to study the habits, calls and field markings of the birds you are likely to spot. Birds often don't hang around, so part of the skill is to be as quick in identifying them as possible.

One might think that bird watchers might be solitary types but nothing could be further from the truth. In fact, 'birders' are a sociable set and the fun of searching and collecting different sightings is increased when you join with others. Search online for local birding groups and chapters.

Local universities and parks may well offer classes or group walks. The more people there are watching and listening, the more birds you'll find, and you will probably meet some interesting and very skilled birders in the process.

As with hunting and hiking, it is important to dress correctly. Colours that blend into your surroundings will help you to stay hidden and avoid alerting birds to your presence.

The best time to begin bird watching is in the morning, when birds are out searching for food. Listening is as important as looking. At this time, the air will be thick with song, though you might not actually be able to see a single bird.

Look for movement in the trees first before bringing the binoculars to your eyes, rather than searching through them.

The alternative to searching for birds is to bring them to you. Erecting bird feeders in your garden is a simple, very effective way to attract them.

(Different types of feed will attract different species, so do some research before you buy, though sunflower seeds are a good bet for a variety of different birds.) You can also install a bird fountain, or shallow water bath, since running and dripping water will attract birds.

In all cases, silence is golden. If you talk loudly, laugh or leave your mobile phone on (duh!), then the birds will likely leave the area before you are able to get close.

Finding, attracting and spotting birds is the first part of the skill, of course, but then you must identify them. It is easy to be misled based on colouring alone, as different species can be similar. Concentrate on the shape and size of the bird instead, as well as its markings, posture and behaviour. Markings will be located on particular parts of the body, such as feathers and tail, etc.

With time and practice, you will come across a wider range of species and, if you're keen, you may decide to start keeping a visual record. This requires a good deal more kit, since you'll need to add a decent camera and tripod and a telescope, but the art of taking good photos of these beautiful creatures adds a new dimension and a new sense of reward to the whole endeavour.

Hardcore 'birders' will travel far and wide in search of sightings missing from their collection (any birder worth the name will have a 'life list') and if you're taken with the sport then you will want to venture further afield. Birds inhabit a fabulous range of environments – mudflats, rivers, fields and forests – and 'birding' offers a great excuse to get out there and discover.

CAMPING

'I would rather own little and see the world than own the world and see little of it' **ALEXANDER SATTLER**

Entire books have been written on the subject of camping and there are different kinds available to cater for each different type of experience. At the top end, you can easily fork out for a set-up that is more akin to a luxury hotel room, with all possible mod-cons available.

However, not only will this put an unwelcome dent in your bank balance but, to our mind, it is at odds with what we consider to be the real purpose of camping: to get out there and get closer to the natural world. What's the fun of escaping if you take modern life, and all its trappings, with you?

What we undertook might best be described as 'minimalist' camping and we found it enriching and (literally) grounding: it is as much about your mindset as it is about the gear you carry.

The object of 'minimalist' camping is to take your cues from the natural world around you as much as possible, rather than your experience being dictated by the kit you have brought.

To get into this spirit, it can be useful to set each camper a bag limit. We decided on one medium-sized bag each, in which we had to accommodate clothes, shoes and bathroom kit (including towel), as well as anything else essential that wasn't part of the campsite set-up itself.

You should be able to carry your bag for a long stretch without needing to put it down. (Trust me: you will be grateful for this during any extended hikes.)

For the campsite itself, you will likely need the following (adjusted to however long you are planning to spend there):

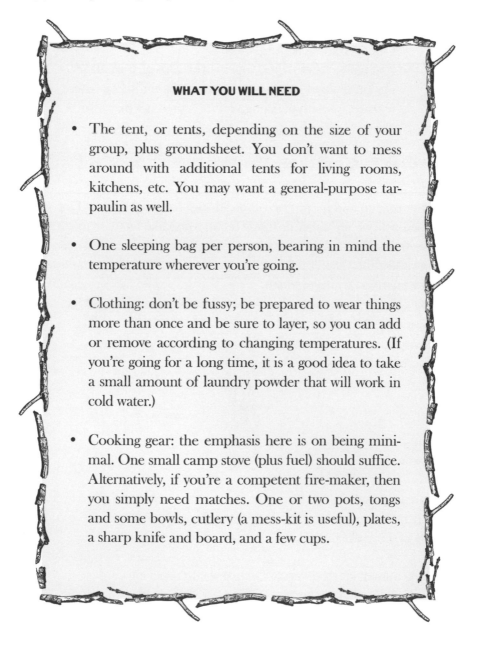

WHAT YOU WILL NEED

- The tent, or tents, depending on the size of your group, plus groundsheet. You don't want to mess around with additional tents for living rooms, kitchens, etc. You may want a general-purpose tarpaulin as well.

- One sleeping bag per person, bearing in mind the temperature wherever you're going.

- Clothing: don't be fussy; be prepared to wear things more than once and be sure to layer, so you can add or remove according to changing temperatures. (If you're going for a long time, it is a good idea to take a small amount of laundry powder that will work in cold water.)

- Cooking gear: the emphasis here is on being minimal. One small camp stove (plus fuel) should suffice. Alternatively, if you're a competent fire-maker, then you simply need matches. One or two pots, tongs and some bowls, cutlery (a mess-kit is useful), plates, a sharp knife and board, and a few cups.

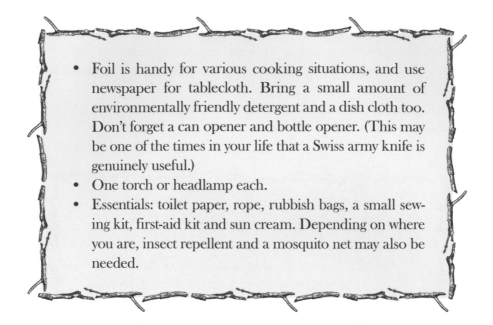

- Foil is handy for various cooking situations, and use newspaper for tablecloth. Bring a small amount of environmentally friendly detergent and a dish cloth too. Don't forget a can opener and bottle opener. (This may be one of the times in your life that a Swiss army knife is genuinely useful.)
- One torch or headlamp each.
- Essentials: toilet paper, rope, rubbish bags, a small sewing kit, first-aid kit and sun cream. Depending on where you are, insect repellent and a mosquito net may also be needed.

Resist the urge to add in 'just one more thing' you might need. Don't do it! The point is to be resourceful. If you're anything like us then you will soon surprise yourself with how much you find you don't actually need. In the bathroom, for instance, a toothbrush, toothpaste, bar of soap and a small bottle of shampoo will be enough.

The same goes for any food that you plan to bring. Starving to death is not the object here but equally you don't want to bring bags full of sauces, seasonings, cans and fancy food that you don't strictly need.

The bare essentials will go far and we found that our senses quickly adapted: it's amazing how supremely delicious something tastes when you've cooked it yourself in the open air.

Assemble a small kit made up of the essential flavourings.

Try to take as little with you as possible: rice, pasta, cooking grains, as well as instant coffee and tea bags, will stretch a long way.

Be resourceful wherever you can: local farms are a great source of fresh fruit and vegetables (which will taste better than something from the supermarket which has been stowed in your rucksack) as well as locally produced meat and milk.

Or, even better, go 'full Rambo' and use the skills you have learned elsewhere in this book to forage and source food.

It is important to be disciplined with yourself about what entertainment you are bringing with you. The idea is to let nature draw you in and that is hard to achieve when you are glued to an iPad. A deck of cards, a swimsuit and a Frisbee are perfect light-to-carry, sociable activities that somehow felt acceptable to us according to our (somewhat arbitrary) minimalist rules.

However, while the purpose of camping is both to discover the great outdoors and also to rediscover some of those joyful activities from which the digital age can distract us – stargazing, storytelling round an open fire, good conversation – there is no need to deny yourself everything. Cameras will allow you to make a record of your experience and document the beauty around you, while a mobile phone (switched to silent) is a sensible safety precaution.

Camping provides a great opportunity to learn about yourself and your companions (in the least wishy-washy sense possible). You will discover levels of resourcefulness and resilience you didn't know you had and you should encourage yourself to learn new ways of doing things and to improvise wherever possible.

If you don't have a clock, then create a sundial. If you don't have a stand for your cooking pots, then improvise and craft one from rocks and logs.

In this way, camping can be a true journey of discovery.

CAMPFIRE COOKING

No matter how spectacular the scenery, a campfire meal is often the highlight of a day spent in the outdoors. After a hard slog through the wilderness, your body cries out for sustenance. And what better way to replenish your reserves than with a meal cooked out under the stars?

The cooking of meat played a central role in the story of our species. Prior to that discovery – probably the result of one of our hapless ancestors dropping his food into the fire by mistake, before realising it tasted extra good – humans, like animals, would have eaten meat raw and suffered any consequences of infection and poisoning that came with it.

However, the real boon of cooked meat was what it did to our brains. Cooking food breaks down its cells, meaning that the body needs to work less hard to extract the all-important nutrients. Put simply, this meant that our guts could shrink while our brains could grow bigger and we were set as a species on the road to becoming the vastly intelligent beings we are now (ha!).

TAKE CARE

In days gone by, cooking on an open fire was a given. Nowadays, however, with concerns about air quality, dwindling firewood and restricted areas for camping, not to mention health and safety, the freedom to cook over an open fire is a privilege, which must be treated with respect and caution.

THERE ARE A FEW IMPORTANT CONSIDERATIONS:

WOOD – To cook on a campfire, you need a clean-burning and very hot fire and this can only be achieved using dry or seasoned (i.e. pre-dried) wood. Stripping green wood from trees is pointless: you will only create a smoky, poorly burning, and polluting fire. If it is damp, then you will need to plan ahead and find somewhere (a campsite or garden centre, for instance) with dry wood. See page 179 for more information on campfire building.

WHERE TO BUILD – Pay close attention to the ground before you prepare your fire. A bed of rock is ideal but if that's not possible you can work on bare mineral soil. If your fire is going to burn for several hours then it will burn through the organic layer of soil in that time. Use previously established fire pits if you can.

WIND – A medium to strong wind is extremely dangerous as it can send sparks flying and potentially cause a forest fire. If you can't find a good wind shelter then you must not go ahead with your fire.

HOW TO BUILD A CAMPFIRE FOR COOKING

You may have an image of roaring flames licking at the grill and turning your burgers to a delicious char but the fact is a successful campfire will be built from wood that has turned into coals. You don't want flames, as they will burn your food and blacken your cookware. Coals will also allow you the longest cooking time.

PREPARE THE SITE

Build your fire at least eight feet from any grass, bushes or anything else that can burn, and be sure there aren't any overhanging branches. Use large rocks or green logs to make a U-shaped border. If you are using logs then you'll need to wet them down now and then. If there is a breeze then the back of your fire pit should face the wind. Place a large, flat rock at the rear of the pit to direct the smoke up and away.

LAY THE KINDLING

Fill the area with crumpled paper or tinder. Lay kindling over the paper in layers, alternating the direction with each layer. Use thin splits of wood or small dead branches. (Do not use the 'teepee style' of laying kindling but stack instead.) Have a bucket of water nearby for safety. Light the paper to start the fire.

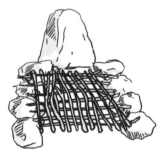

BUILD THE FIRE AND GRADE THE COALS

Once the kindling is ablaze, you need to add firewood. The wood should be all the same size and you want lots. Use hardwoods if you can (such as alder, beech, maple and oak) and distribute evenly over the fire bed.

Once the flames have burned down, leaving mostly white coals, use a stick to rake the coals into a higher level at the back; grading to a lower level at the front. This will give you three areas with high, medium and low heat.

To cook, set your grill on the rock or log sides and watch it sizzle. It is handy to have a small spray bottle or squirt gun to shoot down any unwanted flames caused by fat falling on to the fire. After cooking, add wood to turn it into your evening campfire.

Before going to bed, extinguish the fire thoroughly and soak it with water (see fire-making chapter) and turn the rocks in on the fire bed. This way, the fire can be easily reassembled the following day.

'THOUGHT
IS THE WIND,
KNOWLEDGE THE SAIL,
AND MANKIND THE VESSEL'
AUGUSTUS HARE

ULTIMATE FRISBEE

'You can discover more about a person in an hour of play
than in a year of conversation' **PLATO**

T hink of a Frisbee and you might instantly picture a wobbly plastic disc
rolling uselessly away from you along the grass or arcing silently towards
a forbidding treeline.

However, with a little practice the disc can be thrown with great power and
precision, which makes the game of Ultimate Frisbee – a hybrid of (American) football, soccer, and basketball – a versatile and brilliantly fun game.

According to its inventor, Fred Morrison, the very first Frisbee was a popcorn
lid that he and his girlfriend tossed back and forth to each other. (This was
the 1930s, so people were short on entertainment.) That lid became a cake
pan, which in turn became the disc we know and love.

As with so many of the great sports, Ultimate can be played just about anywhere, provided you have enough space. The object is to get the Frisbee to a
teammate in the 'end zone', without the opposition intercepting.

There is no tackling, so players of different shapes and sizes can team up and
play against each other, without fear of damage to either limbs or friendships.

To play Ultimate, you will need a good amount of room to spread out. Typically it is played on football fields but really it can be played in any open field that's a decent size.

In regulation Ultimate, at each end of the pitch are the end zones, which are 20 yards deep. However, you can simply work with the space you have. So, if you are playing in someone's back yard, just use the proverbial 'jumpers for goalposts' and mark off your own end zones accordingly.

ULTIMATE FRISBEE PITCH

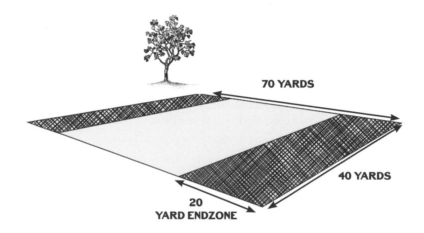

Ultimate is played with two teams. The bare minimum of players would be four in total, with two per team, but that would be beyond challenging. Ideally you want between five and seven players per side. (Regulation Ultimate teams play seven-a-side, with unlimited substitutions to be made any time after a point is scored.)

Really you can play using any type of Frisbee, and you should. (For our game, we used one of those cheap-as-chips versions you find in a string bag in your local newsagent.)

However, those in the know say it is easier to play with a heavier disc, which makes it easier to control your accuracy and distance. 175 gram Frisbees are the official recommended weight.

As with soccer and American football and many other sports where you're aiming at a goal, each team has an end zone that they are defending and one which they are attacking. The object of the game is to pass the Frisbee downfield until you are close enough to attempt a pass into the end zone. There are, however, important rules:

- The player possessing the Frisbee may not move and also may not hold on to the Frisbee longer than ten seconds. During this time, the player's teammates will move around the field, attempting to find space to receive a pass, while the team not in possession will try to intercept the disc and disrupt any passes.
- If the Frisbee is dropped, flies outside the playing area or is intercepted, then possession is handed to the defending team at that place on the pitch.
- To begin play, you must first allocate each team a half (the trusted coin toss comes in handy) and decide which will 'kick off'.

The team kicking off stand in their end zone and 'pull' the disc to the other team, i.e. launch it in the air for someone on the other team to catch. (This will also take place after a point is scored.) Once the Frisbee is launched, the puller's teammates should run towards the opposition to start defending.

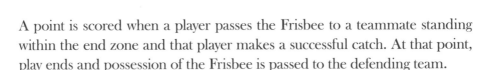

A point is scored when a player passes the Frisbee to a teammate standing within the end zone and that player makes a successful catch. At that point, play ends and possession of the Frisbee is passed to the defending team.

Physical contact is not allowed. Defenders must try to be disruptive and guard the opposing team without actually making contact. It is the job of the defender guarding the player in possession of the Frisbee to count to ten, usually aloud.

A typical game ends when one team reaches 15 points, however that can take up to an hour and a half, so you might want to play to a lower score, or simply stop when more than half the players have wandered off for a drink.

HOW TO THROW A FRISBEE
There are few things more satisfying than chucking the disc a long distance and watching it glide, laser-like, towards its target. And it's not as hard to do as you might think.

The trick is to drink just the right amount beforehand... No, of course it's not, it is, as always, to practise. To throw the Frisbee correctly, place your index and middle fingers beneath the disc, next to the lip.

Get a firm grip by curling the fingers and then twist your body towards your throwing arm side.

Take a step forward with your opposite foot and untwist your body as you do so.

Once you are square on and facing forwards, flick your wrist and let go of the disc at the point where you are aiming, remembering always to keep the Frisbee level with the ground.

TREE CLIMBING

'If growing up means it would be beneath my dignity
to climb a tree, I'll never grow up' **PLATO**

When children look at the world, they often see a playground where we see nothing. There is no purer example of this, we think, than tree climbing. There was a time for us all when a tree represented a magical opportunity to climb towards the heavens – to test your nerve and dare to see the world from a different vantage point.

As with so many things that we might dismiss as 'childish', tree climbing offers the chance to relearn a forgotten skill.

The vast range of trees and the different forms they take makes every climb a unique challenge. Childish pleasure though it may be, tree climbing can be dangerous (you will soon be starkly reminded of just how much heavier you are now than as a carefree youth) and safety must be your first consideration. Find a tree that is sturdy and with good footholds, which you can climb with confidence.

Then you need to bear in mind clothing: you want to wear things that are loose enough to allow you to move freely but not so baggy that you risk getting snagged on branches. For the same reason, do not wear jewellery or accessories.

Ideally, you want to wear shoes that have some flex in them but also good grip. Trainers should be fine but slippery smart shoes are a no-no.

Find a tree with big, strong branches that look as though they will support your weight. (Now is not a good time to be in denial about how much you might have put on over the holidays.) When you first approach a tree, walk round it a few times and do a pre-climb check. Check out the major branches, and visualise your route to the top. Hopefully you will spot some appealing way-points.

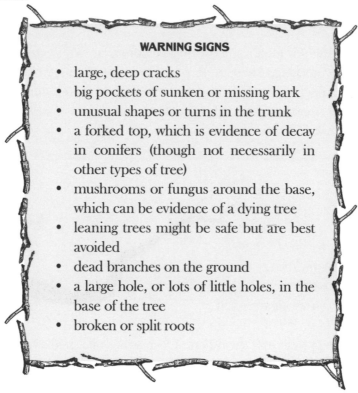

WARNING SIGNS

- large, deep cracks
- big pockets of sunken or missing bark
- unusual shapes or turns in the trunk
- a forked top, which is evidence of decay in conifers (though not necessarily in other types of tree)
- mushrooms or fungus around the base, which can be evidence of a dying tree
- leaning trees might be safe but are best avoided
- dead branches on the ground
- a large hole, or lots of little holes, in the base of the tree
- broken or split roots

Also be mindful of the weather: never climb in a thunderstorm (unless you want to win the Darwin Award), avoid the wet, and bear in mind that cold temperatures can turn wood brittle.

Avoid these local hazards: steer well clear of power lines, do not climb below large branches that are broken or otherwise caught in the tree (hint: they are known as 'widow makers'), look out for wasp nests as well as other birds and mammals, who are likely to be as protective of their home as you would be if some weirdo was trying to climb it.

Begin by finding the tree's lean. To do this, either look at the way the tree is leaning or wrap your hands around it and place your feet on it and see which side you swing towards. Begin your climb, if possible, by gripping the lowest branch with one hand and using your other arm to wrap around the trunk. Either position your foot on a gnarl or use your thighs and calves to grip the trunk between your legs.

Once you have a good hold on the lowest branch, your next move is to get on top of it. If you are reasonably strong, then you may be able to simply haul yourself up. You can do this either by doing a 'pull up', so both biceps and forearms are resting on the branch, at which point you swing and lift to get your elbows on top before swinging your legs round to straddle the branch.

Or, once you have the branch gripped in your hands, swing one leg up over. Now wrap your arms around the branch so that your biceps are on top, before swinging your free leg backwards to gain momentum, then swing yourself on top of the branch.

The object is to climb your way up the tree using the largest, healthiest-looking branches. Once you have scaled a particular branch, look for a safe route to the next one. Grip the branches as near to the trunk as you can. Do not use smaller branches (less than 3 inches/ 7.5 cm wide) for anything more than one limb. And when using branches like this, wedge your foot into the angle where branch meets trunk.

Always avoid dead and/or broken branches, which can break without warning. Similarly, if you notice that the bark is decaying as you climb the tree, then abandon the climb as the tree may not be safe. Trees rot from the inside out, so even if most of the bark looks solid, it could be very dangerous.

Practise what is known in tree-climbing circles as 'triangulation'. This means keeping three limbs in contact with the tree at all times. If one foot is safely in position, so should two hands or arms be. And likewise if two feet are securely in place, then one hand should have a strong hold of a branch.

Do not use the swinging techniques used for reaching the lowest branch during the rest of the climb.

Keep your body as flush to the tree as possible at all times and keep upright, with your hips in a straight line beneath your shoulders. If the tree is narrow enough, then you can wrap your thighs around the side to help with grip, as well as to slow your descent should you fall.

　　　　　TREE CLIMBING

Before you put your weight on any hold, test it first by giving it a hard tug. Do not trust your eyes alone when it comes to the strength of a branch.

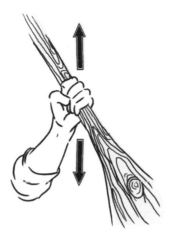

Once you have made good progress you must recognise your limits. Identify how high you can safely climb. Always stop before the trunk narrows to less than 4 inches (10 cm) in thickness and sooner if you can see weak branches or if the wind becomes strong.

Finally, descend with as much care and attention as you used for the climb. Elated though you may be by your success, do not lose your sense of caution, follow the same rules (continue to test each branch, etc.), and keep to the same, tested path that you used on the way up.

FINDING A CLEAN WATER SOURCE

'Water is life, and clean water means health'
AUDREY HEPBURN

Staying well hydrated is of crucial importance while in the wilderness, whether you are hiking, camping or simply spending time outside.

Your body can survive weeks without food, but no more than a day or two without water – it is the lifeblood that our bodies rely on, both to regulate temperature and also to maintain physical performance. This means that after finding shelter, locating a clean source of water is your No.1 survival priority.

Water is heavy and since our bodies require on average a gallon per day in the outdoors, any adventurer worth the name will need to be able to find drinkable water if and when supplies run out.

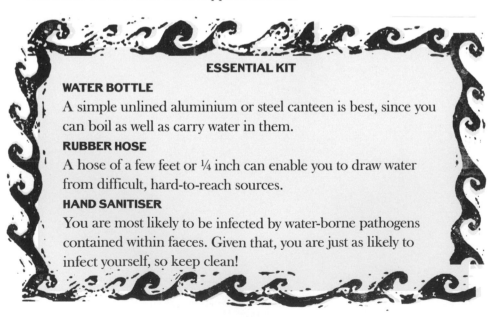

ESSENTIAL KIT

WATER BOTTLE
A simple unlined aluminium or steel canteen is best, since you can boil as well as carry water in them.

RUBBER HOSE
A hose of a few feet or ¼ inch can enable you to draw water from difficult, hard-to-reach sources.

HAND SANITISER
You are most likely to be infected by water-borne pathogens contained within faeces. Given that, you are just as likely to infect yourself, so keep clean!

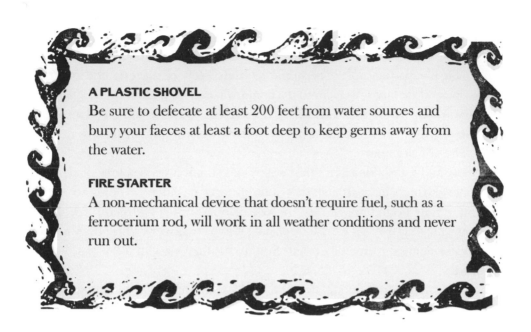

A PLASTIC SHOVEL

Be sure to defecate at least 200 feet from water sources and bury your faeces at least a foot deep to keep germs away from the water.

FIRE STARTER

A non-mechanical device that doesn't require fuel, such as a ferrocerium rod, will work in all weather conditions and never run out.

SELECTING A WATER SOURCE

The single most important piece of advice is to plan ahead. Don't allow yourself to be in a situation where you run out of water or don't know where your next drink is coming from. That way, you won't have to end up drinking your own urine! If you do find yourself in trouble, though, these are the best routes to a clean water source in the wild:

- Clear-flowing water coming from somewhere there aren't people and pollution is best. Streams and springs are ideal filling-up points for your canteen.

- Rivers, ponds and lakes are less ideal. Lakes and ponds are stagnant, which means they might be home to high levels of bacteria and other nasties, while large rivers are often contaminated by pollution.
- Beware any rivers that might have flowed through well-populated areas, construction sites, chemical plants and beneath roads on their way to where you are now.
- Snow and ice (so long as it's freshwater) can supply a good source of clean water during winter, though they should never be eaten, as doing so will lower your body temperature without offering much hydration. Ideally you want to purify snow-melt by placing it in a container with a little water and bringing it to melting point. Simply heating snow in a hot pan will taste vile.
- Sea water and urine should never be drunk (certainly not at dinner parties) but if you are at the point of desperation with no alternatives then they can be boiled. Collect the steam using a plastic bag and allow it to condense.
- Leaves can be a water source, using the same method: wrap branches in a plastic sheet, allowing condensation to form. Use rocks to create low points in the sheet towards which the water will run and can be collected. (Needless to say, don't do this with a poisonous plant.)

- If you aren't able to find a water source, then head downhill (this is also an excellent tip when you're lost) and watch for dark patches in the landscape as well as any clumps of vegetation in a low area, both of which could spell nearby moisture.

PURIFYING THE WATER YOU FIND

Boiling:

This is the single most effective way to rid water of viruses and bacteria. Bring a pan to a roiling boil and keep it there for a minute. This should be enough to make it safe and drinkable.

Filtering:

Filters fall into two types: they either use carbon or ceramic filters that rid the water of contaminants and bacteria, or they treat water with a chemical (often iodine) to kill viruses. The latter is typically cheaper and arguably more reliable.

It can also be wise to filter any water yourself before you treat it by boiling or any other methods. A shirt or a sock can be used in extreme situations, though a paper coffee filter is ideal and makes a very light, very useful addition to your pack.

When using chemicals to treat water, the most affordable and effective method is to add a couple of drops of tincture of iodine. (This is the active ingredient in water purification pills.) Iodine will kill viruses, bacteria and any other harmful things that might be lurking in the water. Bleach works similarly, using just a couple of drops.

Let's say, though, that you have crash landed in the middle of the jungle and have nothing to hand whatsoever. Do not despair. Sunlight can be used as a water purifier. Simply leave a clear water bottle or container in the sun for a full day (if it's sunny) or two days (if overcast) and the sun's UV rays will kill bugs.

If you really are stuck out in the wilderness, though, then the best possible survival rule might be: 'just drink it'. Unless you are standing next to a chemical plant or a sewage works, then the choice between risking infection versus not drinking at all is an easy one. Dehydration will kill you far quicker than bacteria will.

HIKING

'Because in the end, you won't remember the time you spent working in the office or mowing your lawn. Climb that goddamn mountain'

ANONYMOUS

There are few experiences more liberating and thrilling than a good yomp in the outdoors. Travelling on foot allows you to absorb the natural world at the right pace, rather than seeing the countryside flash past your train window or the miles swallowed up on a road trip. Hiking encourages us to notice the natural world: the passing seasons, the wildlife, the way the light falls on the landscape. It truly is a journey of the soul.

For all its transcendent properties, hiking can also be a perilous business if you don't do the proper planning and take precautions as you should.

PREPARATION

The first thing to do is buy a guidebook to the area you are going to be hiking. Local guidebooks can be found online or at local bookshops, and visitor's centres. They will also tell you about the natural landscape around you, including wild flowers and wildlife you are likely to encounter (which, depending on where in the world you are hiking might be an important safety consideration).

The chances are that you are never too far from a good hiking trail, even if you live in the midst of the big smoke.

If you are new to hiking, then begin with a relatively easy trail. There are 'day hikes' that will be manageable for even the novice. You don't want to commit yourself to a hike you can't finish.

Be sure to bring lots of water (more than you think you will need). Staying hydrated is crucial, and you don't want to end up taking any of the drastic – fairly unpleasant – measures covered in this book's chapter on purifying water. A good rule of thumb is to bring at least a litre of water per person for every two hours of hiking you intend to do. If the weather is hot, or the trail especially taxing, then you will need more.

Pack well. Your backpack should carry everything you should and could need during your hike. An energy boosting snack (tradition dictates trail mix if you're American and Kendal mint cake if you're British); a good knife (Swiss army knives are handy); a map and compass; a torch; sun cream; fire-starting equipment; and an extra layer of clothing. It is also advisable to take a first-aid kit, to be safe.

Footwear: never, ever wear flip-flops. They simply won't be up to the task of carrying you and your supplies through rough terrain. Instead, opt for sturdy lace-up boots with good arch support and thick soles. Hiking boots are a great investment. Be sure to break them in before you set off, as bad blisters can be debilitating.

Beginners should avoid hiking alone. If something happens to you, then it is going to be much harder to get help. Ideally, ask someone with experience of hiking to come with you. Failing that, go with friends.

HIKING

If you decide to hike solo, always let someone know where you are going and when you intend to be back.

With safety in mind, a cell phone is essential. If something should go wrong then it could well be your best chance to get help.

SETTING OUT

Hiking trails typically begin with a trail head – this is a sign that will tell you the name of the trail, the distance, and often give a map of your trail and the trails it connects to, as well as highlighting things for you to look out for. Your trail guide should show you where the trail head is located.

Follow the trail markers: you will soon come to a fork in the road of your trail, at which point you must be sure to follow the trail with the correct name (it sounds simple but a tiny mistake like this can send you hours in the wrong direction).

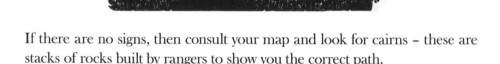

If there are no signs, then consult your map and look for cairns – these are stacks of rocks built by rangers to show you the correct path.

Do not be tempted to do as Robert Frost did and follow the path less travelled. You might see small trails branching off the main track. These are often created by deer and other creatures and can lead you into areas not covered by your map. Often park rangers or other good Samaritans will have blocked off such trails with fallen tree branches.

Hiking is not a good environment in which to explore your non-conformist side: take heed of all signs. If you are told to keep to the path, then it is probably because vegetation is being replanted and your footsteps could cause damage.

Likewise, if you are told not to feed wild animals, then don't. This can be dangerous to both you and them.

'Take only pictures, leave only footprints.'

This is the hiker's mantra and it teaches above all else that the wilderness must be respected and remain untouched by human hand (and foot) as much as possible.

Littering is not yet punishable by death in the UK, though perhaps it should be. Disturbing the peace by shouting and playing loud music must be avoided. And resist the urge to take souvenirs. The true hiker knows above all else to be respectful.

CREATING SHELTER IN THE WILDERNESS

'Build shelter against a rainy day'

JOHN WOODEN

Y ou should always have a good and comfortable tent when you head out into the wild. However, should you ever find yourself in a situation where you are far from help and without shelter as night draws around you, fear not: nature's bounty can provide many of the materials you need.

CREATING A MAKESHIFT TENT

To craft your own tent you will need a rope or line of some sort to hang between two trees; a tarpaulin or poncho to hang from the rope; and something with which to anchor the tarp. The tarp is indispensable; however, if you don't have rope then you can use a thick branch wedged between two trees.

The trees need to be sturdy and ideally located far enough apart that you can comfortably lie in the space between without the rope being stretched too far. To tie your rope, use a type of knot known as a clove hitch, which will secure the rope and stop it from slipping.

CLOVE HITCH

1) Wrap the free end of a rope around a post. 2) Cross over itself and around the post again. 3) Slip working end under last wrap. 4) Pull tight.

CLOVE HITCH

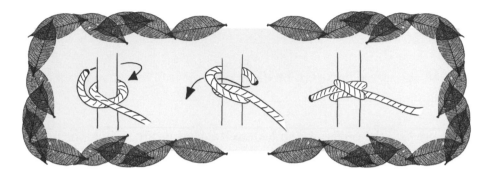

The exception to this is if you are in snowy weather, where you will want your rope to be higher to give the tent steeper sides so it won't collapse under the weight of snowfall.

When you hang your tarp over the line (or branch), it must reach the ground on both sides. Stretch it tight to keep any extra air out of the space.

The edges of the tarp should be secured to the ground using heavy objects, such as large logs or rocks. If you have some extra rope, then create stakes by sharpening sticks and secure the tarp with grommets. Run rope through each grommet to pull the tarp taut and wrap around the stakes you have driven into the ground.

CONSTRUCTING A LEAN-TO

A lean-to is a much simpler construction that needs only a series of branches placed around a large rock or fallen tree.

With the rock or tree in place as your central brace, find some sturdy sticks to form the shelter's sides. Be sure to leave enough space for you to enter between the sticks and the brace.

Keep the lean-to as low to the ground as possible, and out of the way of the wind.

Once the frame is in place, use leaves, grass and moss to form the outside wall of the lean-to. This will keep out the rain, wind and snow as well as keeping you insulated. Pack the debris as tightly as you can to make sure it isn't blown away by the wind.

You can also spread the debris on the floor of the lean-to give you even more insulation.

Dig a fire pit at the centre of your lean-to. Take great care to build the fire far enough away from the sides and roof. Needless to say, if you do build a fire, it must be put out before you go to sleep, or else watched through the night.

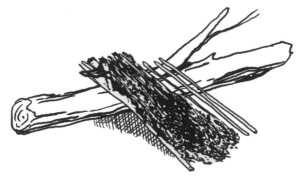

MAKE A DEBRIS HUT

You will need a tree stump or a tree with a low crook that a branch can be lodged into.

A debris hut will keep in heat and keep you warm but it won't be strong enough to withstand any falling objects, so build away from overhanging branches and other hazards.

First, prop a branch against the stump. The branch will need to be near 8 feet in length and sturdy enough to support your body weight. You are going to need to fit in the space beneath.

Find some 'ribbing sticks' to create the frame of your hut. These will need to be long enough to lean against the horizontal branch and get progressively shorter further away from the tree stump. For added strength, you can use rope or twine to bind them in place.

The ribbing sticks should be placed far enough apart so you can fit underneath them. And be sure to lay them so that the sides of the hut are steep enough for water and snow to run off.

With the frame in place, add further sticks perpendicular to the frame to form a latticework. Pile leaves, grass, pine needles and any other debris that you can find on top of this latticework. Ideally you want a layer 3 feet thick on the outside before adding an interior layer for insulation about 6 inches thick.

The drier the debris, the better, and place the driest material nearest to your body on the hut's interior.

With your debris walls in place, layer more branches on top, to help protect against strong winds.

Once finished, enter the hut and close up the entrance behind you with additional debris to trap warmth inside.

Bow & Arrow

'The history of the bow and arrow is the history of mankind'

FRED BEAR

The bow and arrow is older than the history books can fathom. Fragments of the oldest recorded example date to 9000 BC, and it is believed that this lethal weaponry began to spread across the globe at least as far back as the end of the last Ice Age.

Until the invention of gunpowder in the 1500s, the bow and arrow was unmatched both as a weapon of war and as a hunting tool. It has shaped the course of human history perhaps more than any other single technology: from the all-conquering Mongol archers of Genghis Khan to the victorious longbowmen at the Battle of Agincourt. And though it wouldn't be much use to you in a gunfight today, it is still an extremely effective method of hunting and a valuable skill to master.

MAKING THE BOW

The first important step is to find the right wood for your bow. Find a piece of dry and dead hardwood (though not so dead that it has begun to crack). You can, if necessary, use living wood, though it won't provide anything like as much power.

Hardwoods include oak, lemon, hickory, yew and teak. Your section of wood should ideally be about 6 feet in length (1.8 metres) and free of any knots and twists, and thickest at its centre.

It will need to be flexible – woods such as juniper and mulberry are also ideal.

6'

Every piece of wood will have a natural curve. You need to determine this as it will decide where you are going to position the main features of your bow. The simplest way to find the curve is by pinning the wood to the ground at one end while using your other hand to press lightly at its middle. The wood will naturally turn so that its belly faces you.

Next you need to determine the handhold and limbs. First, find the centre point of the bow and make marks 3 inches (7.5 cm) above and below that point. The area within these marks is the handhold.

To shape the bow, place the bottom end on top of your foot and one hand on top of the other end. With the belly (the side curved nearest to you) facing you, use your other hand to press outward against the bow. This will show you where the bow is flexible and where it is not. Use a knife to shave wood away from those points where the bow is not flexing. Continue doing this until both upper and lower limbs of the bow curve an equal amount.

Only carve from the belly and leave your bow thickest at its handhold.

Next, use the knife to cut notches for the bow string. These notches should begin at the sides and curve round toward the belly and in towards the handhold.

There should be one notch on each end roughly 2 inches (5 cm) from the ends of the bow. Remember, never cut into the back of the bow and don't make the notches any deeper than they need to be to hold the string, or they could threaten the bow's integrity.

Your bow string should not be stretchy – it is the wood, not the string, that provides the elastic power. If you don't have string to hand, then you can use fishing line.

Tie a loose loop with a secure knot at both ends of the bowstring before looping it over the lower and then upper limbs of the bow. Your string should be slightly shorter than the length of the unflexed bow, so that when it is attached both the bow and the string are taut.

Next you need to tiller the bow. Hang it from a tree branch so that you can pull downwards on the string. Pull gently to begin with and check that the limbs bend evenly. Carve away any excess wood as required, until you can pull as far as you will need to draw – i.e. the distance between your outstretched hand and your ear.

FOR THE ARROWS

For the arrows, you want to use the straightest sticks you can find. As before, the wood should be dry and dead. An arrow needs to be roughly half the length of the bow.

To shape the arrows, you first need to whittle the wood so that it is smooth around its circumference. An arrow can be straightened by heating it over a fire (taking care not to burn it) before holding the shaft straight while the wood cools.

Carve a notch, called a nock, in the back of each arrow – this is where the bow string will fit.

Next, sharpen the arrow into a point. The simplest arrowhead is a carved point at the front of the shaft. You can do this by whittling a point and then fire-hardening the wood by gently heating it in the coals of a fire.

However, even better is to construct an arrowhead. They can be made from metal, stone, glass or bone. Use a rock or hammer to carefully chip your chosen material into a point. Then, notch the wood of the shaft, insert the arrowhead and bind it in place with string or cord.

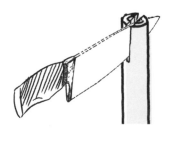  

FOR THE FLETCHINGS

For the best flight and accuracy, you will want to make fletchings, which help the arrow glide through the air. Feathers are traditional and ideal, if you can find them, though you can also use animal fur and even duct tape.

Split the back of the arrow and slide the feather into place, before tightly wrapping a thin thread (use your own clothing if necessary) around the fletching.

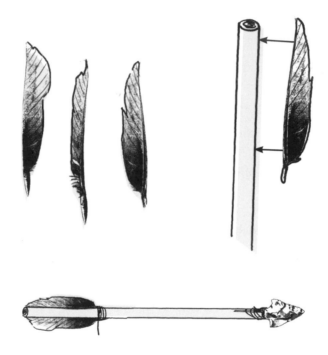

BUILD A SANDCASTLE

'Like a sandcastle, all is temporary. Build it, tend it, enjoy it.
And when the time comes, let it go' **JACK KORNFIELD**

Who needs an overly muscled body? If you want to be the true king of the beach then you'll need to know how to build a killer sandcastle, complete with towers and moat.

The golden rule of building is to always use moist sand. This is the building block of any decent structure. You can test moisture by squeezing a ball of sand in your hand for a few seconds – if the ball stays together as you roll it around your palm then it's perfect. You don't want it to crumble to pieces, nor to be so sopping wet that it falls through your fingers. The place to find good sand is below the tide line.

The favoured recipe for 'castle concrete', as it's known, is one part sand to one part water. Using a big bucket, pour the water in first before mixing in the sand thoroughly.

To get the right density, build your mound of sand slowly by adding six inches of sand at a time, before packing it down firmly with your fists and pouring half a bucket of water over it. (Don't ever worry about adding too much water, as any excess will just drain off.) Continue this process until you have reached your desired height.

At the beach, the best way to get an unlimited supply of water is to dig a hole that will continue to replenish. Just keep digging until water starts puddling at the bottom.

EQUIPMENT

The best sand sculptors avoid plastic buckets or other closed moulds and instead build their shapes by stacking handfuls of wet sand and tamping it down.

You can successfully build a castle using nothing but your bare hands, however having the right tools will make the whole process much more enjoyable.

Here are the must-have items...

A LIGHTWEIGHT SHOVEL WITH A LONG HANDLE

As your castle climbs higher and higher, you will need to dig deeper and deeper. Digging for sand is the most exhausting part of the process and a good shovel will make light work of it.

AT LEAST TWO BUCKETS

One in which to mix the sand and water, and one to carry the water from the hole.

TOOLS FOR CARVING

Many of these can be sourced from your kitchen and/or tool box. At the very least you will need a kitchen, or plastic, knife with the tip removed. The best shaping tool will be something with an offset handle – a pastry knife with a squared-off end is ideal.

FINISHING TOOLS

You will need a soft-bristled paintbrush for smoothing surfaces and a drinking straw for blowing away excess sand. (Short of any of the above, a decent set of tools can be crafted from plastic eating utensils.)

HOW TO BUILD

The trick used by the masters of the craft is a technique known as 'hand-stacking'. The big difference versus the kind of sandcastle-building most of us are used to is that instead of pounding the dry sand into place and then adding water, you instead allow a pre-mix of sand and water to fall into place under its own weight.

1. First, use your hands (and feet) to mix the compacted sand and water at the bottom of your water hole. It should have the consistency of cake batter. Keep the mixture moving throughout the build, otherwise the water and sand will naturally separate.

2. Scoop large handfuls of the mixture. It is easier to work big rather than small to start with.

3. Next, plop the mixture on to your base in one smooth motion. Resist the urge to slam it into place. The taller your castle gets, the gentler you will need to be. If you are building a tower, then your hands should be on top, and if you are building a wall your hands will go to the sides.

4. Gently jiggle the new pile of sand. You want the new layer of sand to melt into the layer beneath. Again, resist the urge to pound or slam. Instead, by vibrating the new sand gently you are encouraging it to settle evenly across the layer beneath. Jiggle until the sand stops flowing. Any longer and cracks will form.

THE STRUCTURES

Sandcastles are made up of three basic building units: the tower, the wall, and the arch. Your ability to grow your castle will be limited only by how moist you can keep the sand and how large your base is in diameter.

TOWERS

Once you have piled the sand that will form your foundation and smoothed its surface flat, scoop a large double-handful of sand on to the foundation. Flatten it in place using your palms. You want the patty of sand to be 20–30cm in diameter. Remember to keep working the sand with a constant jiggling action and be quick, otherwise the water will run away before the sand is in position. And be sure to stop jiggling once the water has run off, to avoid cracking the sand.

Continue this process. As the tower gets taller, you will apply less pressure to flatten the sand and spend more time jiggling. Each successive layer, or patty, should be slightly smaller than the one beneath to stop it from overspilling. The very top layers don't need to be jiggled, just gently placed.

Continue until the tower begins to look precarious. Then move on to the next one.

20–30 CM

WALLS

Walls can be used to surround your castle, connect towers together and even create staircases.

The process of building walls is essentially the same as for towers, except you first need to form the sand mixture into bricks.

After plopping the mixture into place between two of your towers, you will need to move your hands to the sides and jiggle until it fills the space between your hands. To do this, keep your hands flat with palms parallel to each other and facing inward about 10 cm apart. (Be careful not to jiggle the towers as you do this.)

BUILD A SANDCASTLE

With one brick in place, repeat the process on top of that, and continue until all of your towers are connected by walls.

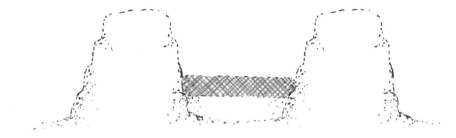

ARCHES

Building an arch is not as complicated as it might seem, and once you have mastered the positioning of the keystone you will have the knack.

To begin with, you might want to experiment by tunnelling through a wall. Once you are comfortable doing that, you will be ready to try building an arch. Start by building two towers about 10 cm apart. Once you have reached the height at which you want the arch to begin, scoop a handful of wet sand on to one of the towers and slop it over the edge towards the other tower. Do the same on the other tower.

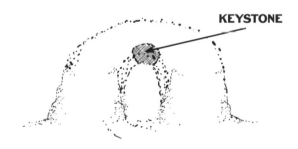

KEYSTONE

Continue this process, each time building upwards and outwards to bring the two ends closer together. You will have to build up as well as out, or the tower will fall. When the two ends are very close you add one final plop of sand (the keystone), which will hold the ends together.

You can add layers of sand on top of the arch to achieve the required level of thickness. Just be sure not to pack the sand into place but, as ever, let the liquid sand settle by jiggling it gently.

BRING IT ALL TOGETHER

With your towers in place, however many you want, you need to connect them up with the walls, bridges, arches and staircases.

DECORATION

The basic rules of carving are, as above, to always work your way down the sandcastle and continue to blow away excess sand as you go.

Keep your knife at a constant angle, so it shaves and smooths the surface and remember to work gradually.

PÉTANQUE

'I had no chance of controlling a ball game until I first controlled myself'

CARL HUBBELL

There is perhaps no game that so immediately summons the feeling of a blissful Provençal holiday than petanque.

Originally played by the Romans (aiming a thrown object at a fixed point on the ground is a game almost as old as civilisation itself), it has become a signature of the region. With a glass of pale rosé in hand and the gentle metallic 'clink' of the balls sounding in your ears, this is an eminently pleasing game.

Many countries around the world play a descendant of the game that began as *boules* – it was first *bocce* for the Italians, 'bowls' for the English and 'bowling' for the Americans. Pétanque, as we know it now, is thought to have originated near Marseille in 1910. The word *pétanque* comes from the word *petanca*, which in the Provencal dialect means 'feet planted', and this is a defining feature of the game.

HOW TO PLAY

The object is to stand within a circle drawn on to the ground (typically the game is played on a dirt or gravel surface) and roll or lob your ball as close as possible to the target ball, known as the *cochonnet*. Only the winning team in each round scores any points, and the first team to reach 13 wins.

First, divide into two teams. You can play with 1 to 3 people on each team. With 1 or 2 people per team, each player gets three balls, whereas with 3 on each team each player gets only two balls.

Flip a coin to see which team throws first, whereupon the starting team draws a circle in the ground before throwing the *cochonnet* a distance of between 6 and 10 metres (19.7 to 32.8 feet).

The starting team throws their first *boule*, aiming to get as close to the *cochonnet* as possible.

The second team then throw their first *boule*, trying to get closer than the first team. (They are allowed to knock the first team's *boule* aside to do this.)

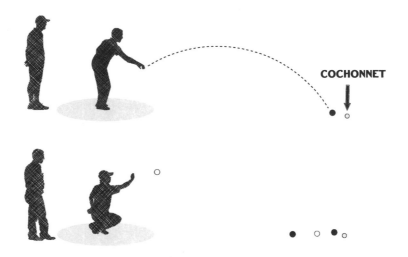

COCHONNET

The teams take it in turns to attempt to get their *boules* closest. Crucially, only the team with the nearest *boule* will score any points. This is called 'having the point'.

Once all the *boules* have been thrown, the team which 'has the point' will score however many *boules* are closer to the *cochonnet* than the opposing team's nearest *boule*.

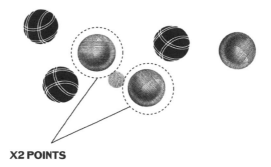

X2 POINTS

The team which 'had the point' on the previous round draws a circle around the position of the *cochonnet* and uses that as the next throwing circle. The teams continue to 13 points.

HOW TO THROW

There is no single correct way to throw a *boule*, and the pros use a range of techniques. However, there are a few tips to improve your accuracy.

Stance – both feet must be in contact with the ground for it to be a legal throw. Generally speaking, you want to stand with your feet a bit less than shoulder- width apart and, if necessary, with one foot slightly in front of the other for stability.

Grip – you want to generate some back spin to control the amount the ball rolls when it lands. The best way to do this is using an underhand technique, which can feel a bit strange to begin with. Hold out your playing hand palm upwards and curl the *boule* in your fingers around your palm. Your fingers should gently touch each other, though your thumb should be off to the side.

Now turn your hand over, so the *boule* hangs in your hand. Keep your hand as relaxed as possible and avoid gripping too tightly.

Swing – with the *boule* securely cupped in your hand, rotate your arm backwards from the shoulder joint and swing back like a pendulum. Practise the feel of swinging a few times. When ready, crouch as low as you comfortably can and release the *boule* from your hand at the forward point that feels right. The motion of the *boule* against your fingers as it is released will naturally give it backspin. Keep the line of your swing as constant as possible, and avoid throwing across your body.

FREERUNNING/PARKOUR

'I deal with challenges the same way I deal with obstacles in Parkour.
I overcome them' **BASILIO 'QUIET' MONTILLA**

Originally known as 'Art du Déplacement', what we now know as Parkour or Free Running began in France in the 1980s. The idea is to train the body to move freely over and through any (typically urban) terrain. By running, jumping and climbing your way round a series of obstacles, you train your body and mind to be as effective and free-ranging as possible in any environment.

Although it involves some spectacular movements, Parkour is not about being a daredevil and putting yourself at risk. On the contrary, safety is paramount and the most effective free runners will be mindful of their limits and commit to getting better with steady practice.

The first great advantage of parkour as a sport is that to do it you really need nothing much more than your body. You need neither special equipment nor a particular place in which to practise. Your body is your only tool and the world around you is your arena.

You will, however, need a good pair of lightweight shoes with decent grip and cushioning to absorb shock. Do not wear football boots or skateboarding shoes. A shoe with a flat sole which fits well will serve you best.

No special clothing is required, though you will need to move quickly and without restriction. Avoid jeans, as they are likely to be too stiff. Cotton is a good idea, to help you keep cool.

To begin with, your hands are going to get scuffed. Resist the urge to buy gloves, though, as your sense of touch will be helpful to your climbing. Your skin will soon toughen up.

Find a training ground – parkour is traditionally an urban sport, but you can just as easily find good obstacles on which to practise your skills in the countryside. A park can be an ideal place to begin, as grass will cushion your fall as you learn. Needless to say, steer clear of private property unless you want to end your practice session in the back of a police van.

Parkour is first and foremost about being in good physical condition, which is one of the reasons it's so worthwhile. So it's a good idea to get yourself in shape early on. Hit the running machine, swimming pool or squash court to get your aerobic fitness to a good level. You won't be able to run, jump or climb well if you're constantly short of breath.

Once your lungs are up to scratch, turn your attention to improving your muscles. Again, you don't need any equipment. Use your own body weight by doing push-ups, pull-ups, squats and leg lifts to build and condition your muscles. And remember to rest – muscle work every other day is a good rule of thumb.

The key to any exercise regime is not to rest on your laurels. Once you are comfortable running a particular distance or doing a number of sets of reps, you need to increase the workload to avoid plateauing.

LEARNING THE MOVES

Remember, begin slowly: if you overreach and injure yourself, then you will set yourself back indefinitely. Only attempt what you know you are capable of and continue to practise until you are confident. Respect your body.

Know your limits: how high and far can you jump? How flexible are you?

LANDING

Parkour is built around a basic landing. The principles of this technique will be used for more advanced techniques, so it's important to master it. There are four key elements to this landing:

1. Land with your legs evenly spaced – roughly shoulder-width apart.

2. Land on the balls of your feet. This enables your body to act like a spring and distribute the energy of the landing. If you land on your heels, you risk injuring your joints.

3. Do not bend your knees beyond 90 degrees – this will slow you down and put too much pressure on your joints.

4. When landing from a higher drop, or when carrying forward momentum, allow your hands to ground and absorb some of the energy. This will also help you to keep your knees from over-bending.

1.

2.

3.

4.

THE SHOULDER ROLL

This is a simple but essential tool for parkour. The shoulder roll reduces the impact of a landing by converting the downward motion into forward motion, allowing you to continue running. The principle is to forward-roll diagonally across your back over your shoulder (reducing the chance of damage to your back and spine).

The idea is to roll on your shoulder, diagonally across your back, so you're rolling from one shoulder through to the hip on the other side of your body. Keep your head tucked beneath your armpit as you enter the roll. Try to 'round' your body get yourself into a ball. As your weight carries you through the roll, stay in this tuck, keeping knees bent, weight low to the ground, as you get back to your feet.

Use vaults to help you practise the art of clearing obstacles and keeping your motion as you land.

Using a rail, run up to it and, as you approach, position your hands and swing your legs to your favoured side. As your knees swing up over the rail, you need to clear your arm out of the way.

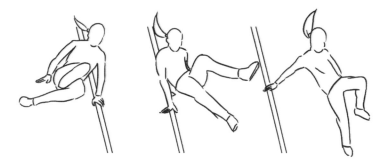

Once you are confident doing it that way, switch to the other side of your body.

JUMPING

Begin jumping from a height lower than you reach when you jump. A good idea is to start from some steps and gradually work your way up as you gain confidence. You should be able to land consistently on your toes with your body relaxed and balanced. Once you can do that time after time without fail, progress to the next step.

PULL-UPS

In order to be able to climb up and over walls, you will need to develop the muscles you use to do pull-ups. The best way to practise is to find a bar that has a good amount of room above it.

Start with a normal pull-up, i.e. to the point where your elbows are in line with the bar, and progress to bringing your chest up and over. Ultimately you want to be able to bring your arms straight over the bar, so that it rests near your hips.

This will help develop muscles used in getting over walls and vaulting objects.

With time and practice, you may want to tackle the 'cat leap', which is a kind of combination of a jump and a climb. The cat leap is useful when you want to jump a gap which is too high above you for you to land on your feet. Instead, you hang from the wall with your hands.

Once you are hanging from the edge of the wall, pull yourself up by bringing your knees into your chest and using your toes to press against the wall. Use your toes to drive your legs up and at the same time use your hands to pull you up. Your legs are more powerful and will do the bulk of the work here.

Once your shoulders have cleared the top of the ledge, spread your hands so that your palms are flat against the surface and straighten your arms, pushing up your body. Lean your weight forward, so that you are pulled towards the safe side.

HENRY DAVID THOREAU

'In wildness is the preservation of the world'

Throughout this book there are various quotes from Henry David Thoreau. This is because Thoreau, the poet, political agitator, philosopher, transcendentalist, gardener and all-round great mind might reasonably be considered the father of environmentalism and one of the greatest thinkers on what it means to be 'wild'.

Of all the major poets of the 19th-century, it is Thoreau perhaps who speaks most directly to our modern condition of restlessness and a feeling that the daily grind of work has taken us away from nature and our true purpose in life. One of Thoreau's most memorable lines says that 'The mass of men lead lives of quiet desperation' – something that might resonate with those of us who feel overwhelmed by modern life.

Born in Concord, Massachusetts in 1814, Thoreau was diagnosed with tuberculosis at a young age (a disease that would eventually kill him). Perhaps it was Thoreau's sense of his own mortality that drove him constantly to seek out a different, more spiritually oriented way of life. His best known work, *Walden, or Life in the Woods*, espouses a life lived in the wild, away from the restrictions of urban living and the habits of a meagre workaday existence.

The book was written at Thoreau's house, Walden Pond, in Massachusetts, which he had built himself on land belonging to his great friend and another poetic master of the age, Ralph Waldo Emerson. While living there, Thoreau made the deliberate choice to immerse himself in the natural world around him.

While other great writers of his time have since faded into history, Thoreau remains as relevant today as ever, as someone who questioned the ways of modern life and who saw a better way of life for us all in the natural world.

A way of living where we would re-connect with nature and remember how to lead a deliberate life.

BEGINNING A GARDEN

'To plant a garden is to believe in tomorrow'
AUDREY HEPBURN

There are lots of good reasons to get into gardening. It is both economical and ecological to grow your own food, it is great exercise (ten minutes with a spade will have your biceps singing) and it is a reason to get out into the wild when the weather would have others huddling around a radiator. Above all, though, from the moment we plant a seed, gardening intimately connects us with our planet. It reminds us, as nothing else, of our place in the natural world. The way that you look at the trees, the birds, the light, the drops of dew on the ground will be forever changed. In an ever-more frantic world, a garden invites us to take precious pause.

When to start? Springtime is the most obvious opportunity to begin a garden, though you can start making plans before the snow has melted. Summer is typically the time for watering, weeding and watching young plants grow. Autumn is a good time to plant shrubs, bulbs, perennials and trees.

All gardens begin with an idea. What sort of garden is this going to be? A vegetable garden? A herb garden? A flower garden? If it is to be a flower garden then do you want annuals? (They will need to be replanted each year but will offer beautiful colours in the summer.)

Or perennials, which bloom for a shorter time but which will return year after year? Of course, you can mix and match – this is your garden.

However, it's a good idea to begin small as you get the habit.

Next you need to pick a place. Bear in mind what you are growing – almost all vegetables and flowers need six hours or so of full sun each day. Spend a day in your chosen garden spot and observe how the sun moves through the space. Also bear in mind the type of soil in your garden, whether it is heavy and clay or light and sandy. If you aren't sure what kinds of plants will work best, you can take your cue from nearby gardens. If your spot is mainly sunless, you can select plants that tolerate shade.

You can find information on plant tags and also ask staff at garden centres. Don't plant shrubs too near to fences or walls as they will grow outwards as well as upwards.

Choose a garden somewhere you can't ignore it – in your back garden near the door, somewhere you like to sit and think, even a box on your kitchen windowsill. Place it near enough a water source that you won't need a super-long hose or have to ferry a watering can a long way.

Prepare the ground. Remove any sod and weeds from the area you are planning to plant. It typically takes around four months for the compost and newspaper to decompose.

Boost the soil. Usually soil needs to be improved by adding organic matter. Add a 2- to 3-inch layer of compost, decayed leaves, and/or manure and till it into the soil. If you are working with an established bed that you can't dig, then you can leave the organic matter on the surface and it will work its way into the soil within a few months.

Dig for victory. Digging loosens up the soil, allowing roots to find their way more easily. However, don't dig when the soil is either too wet or too dry, or it will damage the structure. The soil should be moist enough to form a ball when you squeeze it in your palm.

Use a spade or fork to gently turn over the top 10 inches or so of soil, mixing in the organic matter mentioned above. For vegetable gardens and beds with annual flowers, the soil should be turned only once a year, in the spring, before planting.

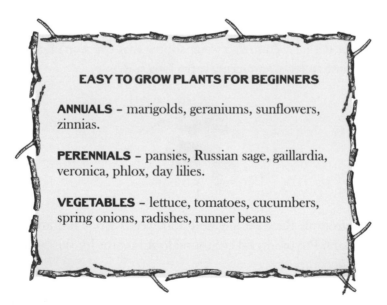

Select your plants. The most important thing to bear in mind is which plants will work with your climate and soil type as well as the amount of sunlight that your garden gets. Your local garden centre will be helpful, but here are some useful suggestions:

EASY TO GROW PLANTS FOR BEGINNERS

ANNUALS – marigolds, geraniums, sunflowers, zinnias.

PERENNIALS – pansies, Russian sage, gaillardia, veronica, phlox, day lilies.

VEGETABLES – lettuce, tomatoes, cucumbers, spring onions, radishes, runner beans

ANNUALS  **PERENNIALS**

Plants such as lettuce and sunflowers can easily be grown from seed and you can sow them directly in the garden. The seed packets will tell you when to plant, how deep to plant and how far apart they should be planted. If you're keen to get started early, you can begin sowing indoors before the frost ends, using containers for seedlings. Be delicate when handling your seedlings and new plants. Don't pull them from their pots by their stems, as they can easily break. Instead, gently squeeze the sides of the pot and turn it upside-down to release them.

Place containers on a sunny windowsill and keep the seedlings moist but not too wet, or they could rot. Hang on to any and all labels as they are going to be essential reminders to you as your garden begins to grow. Be sure to label everything – a large pack of labels and waterproof marker pen are great investments.

Alternatively, you can buy young plants, which can be transplanted straight into the ground. If you are doing this then it is essential to first soak the roots of the young plants before you place it in the soil. Be sure to dig the hole a wider circumference than the roots of the plant – the roots will need to grow to be able to capture the essential moisture and nutrients from the soil.

Give your plants the space that they need. Young plants placed too close to each other won't survive and will also be more susceptible to disease. Your plants' labels should advise on how far apart they need to be planted.

WATER

Seedlings and plant transplants should be watered daily to begin with, but will need less and less as they grow into larger plants. It will depend on your climate, i.e. how humid or not it is and the amount of rain you get, but if your plant wilts in the heat during the day then it is crying out for water. Water slowly and mindfully. Remember that plants have evolved to draw the moisture they need from the environment and not from daily irrigation. To help you gauge the right moisture level, stick your fingers into the soil surrounding the plant and only water if it feels very dry.

MULCH

To protect the soil from weeds and to help lock in moisture, cover the soil with two inches or so of mulch. For annuals or a vegetable garden you want a mulch that will decompose in a few months. Perennials will need longer-lasting mulch such as bark chips.

Stay involved. More than anything else, your garden needs love and attention. Water regularly, pull out any weeds and fertilise (about halfway through the season with a dry fertiliser and every month if using a liquid fertiliser). Indeed, adopt a zero-tolerance policy to weeds as they represent the single biggest threat to your garden. Weed religiously and take care to remove their roots.

A well-loved garden will more than return the amount you invest in it.

FOLK DANCING

'Let your life lightly dance on the edges of time like dew on the tip of a leaf'
RABINDRANATH TAGORE

A lmost every culture around the world has a form of folk dancing to its name. As a cultural expression, dancing is unparalleled; it predates the written word and perhaps even language itself as a method of communication among people. Music, rhythm and movement are a universal language, but one with which many of us in the West have lost contact.

There is something transcendent about giving yourself to music and allowing your body to find a rhythm and a beat. The beauty of the ceilidh dance, which has its origins in Celtic culture, is that as with many folk dances it calls for a group of people to fall in together and lock arms. It creates an extraordinary communal spirit. And if you've ever done it at a wedding you'll know it's also a great way to burn off food and booze!

Fast-paced and easy to learn, 'Strip the Willow' is among the most popular of all the folk dances.

This dance is typically performed by groups of eight people to the bars of the music as below.

First, each dancer must find a partner and face each other, so that the dancers form into two lines, (traditionally this would be one line of men and one of women).

FOR BARS 1 – 8
Starting from nearest the band, the first couple link arms and do a spin.

FOR BARS 9–20

This first lady then 'strips' (i.e. dances her way down) the line of men. With her left hand she takes the hand of each of the men on the line in turn (2, 3, and 4). In between each one of these spins, she uses her right hand to spin her partner, until she reaches the end of the line.

FOR BARS 21–4

Having reached the end of the line, the first couple link their arms and spin.

FOR BARS 25–36

The man 'strips' his way in the other direction, going back up the line towards the band. With his left hand, he turns first the fourth lady, then the third and then the second, all the while using his right hand to spin his partner between each turn.

FOLK DANCING

FOR BARS 37–40

The first couple then spin again at the top of the line, near the band.

FOR BARS 41–52

Then the first couple each 'strip' down their side of the line, as before using their left hand to spin down the line and their right hand to spin their partner in between each time.

FOR BARS 53–56

The first couple come to a stop at the bottom of the line, leaving the second couple at the top of the line, ready to repeat the entire process. Continue until all four couples have had their turn.

TREE SWING

'One can never consent to creep when one feels an impulse to soar'

HELEN KELLER

Tree swings provide a magical moment in childhood; we can remember the dangerous thrill of going higher and higher while at the same time feeling completely safe in the hands of your parent. And a good rope swing can be a joyful thing for an adult too, feeling the air rush past as you soar towards the sky or whiling away the time in the dappled shade engrossed in a book.

The most important safety considerations when building a tree swing are the strength of the branch and the quality of the rope.

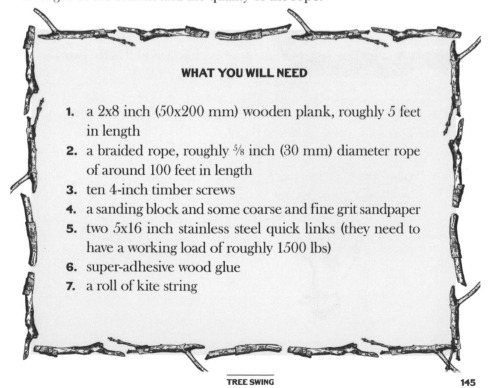

WHAT YOU WILL NEED

1. a 2x8 inch (50x200 mm) wooden plank, roughly 5 feet in length
2. a braided rope, roughly ⅝ inch (30 mm) diameter rope of around 100 feet in length
3. ten 4-inch timber screws
4. a sanding block and some coarse and fine grit sandpaper
5. two 5x16 inch stainless steel quick links (they need to have a working load of roughly 1500 lbs)
6. super-adhesive wood glue
7. a roll of kite string

The rope we used had a working load of 1500 lbs, which should be more than ample for a couple of adults to use at once.

Use a larger-diameter braided rope, if possible, rather than a narrower or twisted rope. This will help to prevent the rope from slipping on the chain link and also stop the seat from tipping.

Nylon is even stronger and better as a rope material than the hollow-core polypropylene rope we used but it is more expensive. Your local hardware shop should be able to advise you.

TOOLS
1. cordless drill
2. pen
3. carpenter's square
4. wood saw
5. a spirit level
6. steel tape measure
7. cigarette Lighter

BUILDING THE SEAT

The seat we made is 40 inches long by 2 inches by 9 inches and was made from pressure-treated (strong) lumber. (Again, ask at your hardware shop for advice.)

The seat reinforcements are made from two 4-inch-long pieces of 2x8.

First, use a pen to mark before sawing the bench seat as well as the two 4-inch reinforcement blocks.

Use the sandpaper to round off the front and rear edges of the seat so the edges won't cut into your legs when you sit.

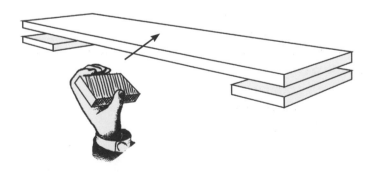

Attach the reinforcing blocks to the outside edges underneath the seat, using the wood glue and the five 3-inch wood screws. Be sure to position the screws so they avoid the holes you are going to drill for the rope.

Mark and drill the ¾-inch (19mm) diameter holes for the rope a couple of inches from the outside end of the seat and slightly less far than that from the front and back sides.

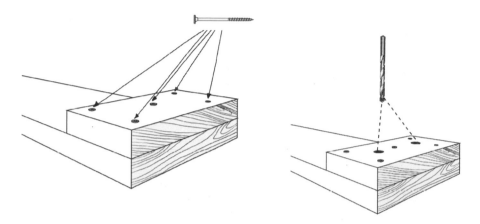

TYING THE ROPE TO THE TREE LIMB

Depending on how high your chosen branch is, you may need to use an extension ladder. If so, take extra care, read all the safety instructions and enlist the help of a friend to steady the ladder as you climb.

We used a running bowline knot to secure the rope to the branch. The advantage of this knot is that it can be tied off from the ground, meaning you won't need to reach your arms around the branch. It is also a 'slipknot', which means that it will expand as the tree grows.

RUNNING BOWLINE

STEP 1 – First make a a double loop.

STEP 2 – Tuck the working end of the rope under and through the two loops.

STEP 3 – Wrap the working end around the standing part of the rope before bringing it down through the double loops.

STEP 4 – The working end is then tucked into the hole made by the double loops.

STEP 5 – Pull on both ends to draw the knot tight, leaving a small loop of a few inches at the bottom.

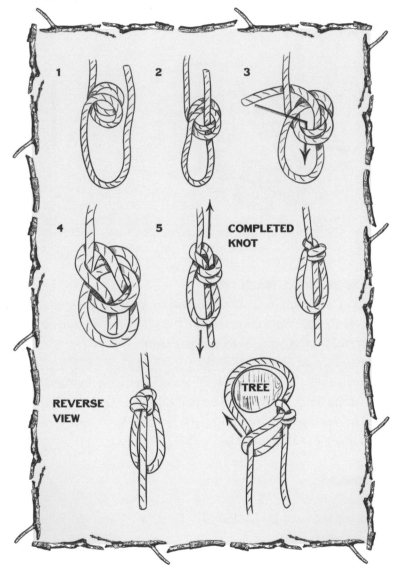

After throwing the rope over the tree limb, the standing part of the rope is tucked through the loop of the bowline knot. The knot slides up snug around the tree limb as the rope is pulled from the ground.

TREE SWING

This makes it easy if tying the rope over a high tree branch that can't be reached from the ground.

If you can't reach the limb with a ladder, use a small rock tied to a spool of kite thread tied to the rope and throw it over the limb. With the kite string looped over the branch, you tie the free end of the kite string to the rope and pull it back up over the limb. You will need a double length of rope for this.

Next, tie a running bowline knot in the rope and pull it so it is held securely up against the limb.

Do this for both ropes.

With both ropes hanging from the tree, carefully use a sharp knife to cut them at the ground.

Remember that you need twice the length of rope to drape it over the tree limb and run the bowline knot up to reach the branch.

SECURING THE ROPE TO THE SWING SEAT

Measure a length of rope of 10–15 feet and pull each end through the holes you have made in the seat. For this we used an 'ashley stopper knot', which is well suited to the task because it is bulky, has a large load-bearing area that's perfect for the seat.

ASHLEY'S STOPPER

STEP 1 – Make a loop in the rope, then pull the inside loop through the top loop to catch it.

STEP 2 – Pull the inside loop through the knot.

STEP 3 – Tuck the working end of the rope beneath the inside loop and then through the top loop.

STEP 4 – Before you pull the ends tight, the knot should look like this.

STEP 5 – Pull the ends tight to close up the knot.

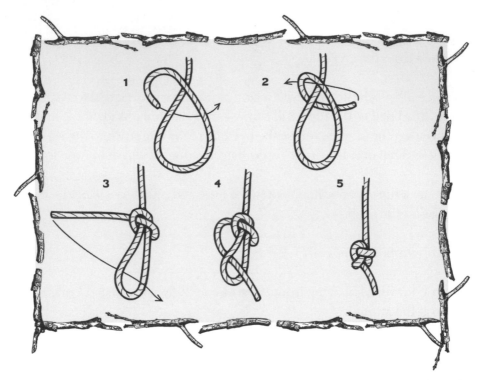

Do the same for the opposite end of the seat, using another 10-foot length of rope.

Adjust the position of the second knot to draw the seat level and leave a short 'pigtail' in each knot for added safety.

FINAL ASSEMBLY

Install one of the quick links on each of the seat rope loops.

Play with the amount of slack, so that the seat is about 25 inches above the ground. Tie the rope that is hanging from the tree to the quick link using a knot known as a 'buntline hitch'.

BUNTLINE HITCH

STEP 1 – Tuck the rope into the metal link.

STEP 2 – Wrap the working end of the rope around the standing part, as pictured.

STEP 3 – Make a Figure 8.

STEP 4 – Tuck the working end of the rope through the bottom of the Figure 8 to create a half-hitch knot.

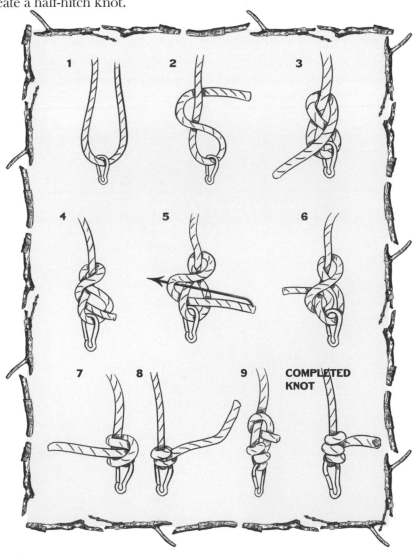

STEP 5 – Bring the working end back and pull it through to create a second Half-Hitch.

STEP 6 – You now have two half-hitches.

STEP 7 – Pull on the rope tight so it closes up the knot.

STEP 8 – Bring the working end of the rope over to the right.

STEP 9 – To be triple-safe, tie a third half-hitch knot and pull it taut.

- Use a lighter to melt the ends of the rope and seal the braids so it won't unravel.

ROCKPOOLING

'The world's finest wilderness lies beneath the waves'
CARLOS M. DUARTE

There is a world beneath the waves that is every bit as awesome and diverse as the land above it. With 71 per cent of the Earth's surface covered in water, there are unnumbered mountains, caves, plains and dunes lying in wait below, each host to species of flora and fauna.

Short of chartering a boat, rockpooling offers us the best opportunity to peak at this other world. And when the tide is out and the waves have made their temporary retreat, we can get a glimpse into this strange and fascinating kingdom.

Rockpooling is an adventure for both young and old. In the UK crabs, shrimps, anemones, limpets, snails and starfish can all be found around the coast.

If you get it right, you might find spiny urchins, starfish as big as your forearm, perfectly camouflaged fish and even the live egg cases of small sharks.

You can go rockpooling at any time of year, really, though late spring or early autumn is best, as the weather is kinder. In the UK, the seas will be warmest around September and coldest in March.

Aim to start an hour or two before low tide, so that you can get further out and not risk being cut off – the best place to be is near the tide.

With calm weather the surface of the water will be more still and you will be better able to see what lies beneath.

Be sure to wear shoes with a good amount of grip. An old pair of trainers with a thick sole or wellington boots are ideal.

And take warm clothing – you should be prepared to do a fair amount of standing around in cold weather.

A small first-aid kit is also a wise addition, to deal with any cuts and scrapes on the rocks. Beaches slope downwards, so the further towards the sea you go, the deeper the underwater habitat you'll be exploring. Start your rockpooling as far down the beach as you can to find some amazing creatures. You can work back up the beach as the tide comes in.

Look under rocks and overhangs. Sea creatures like to stay cool and damp, so you're not going to find many by looking on exposed rocks.

Look deep into pools, crevices and holes in the rock and gently lift stones and seaweed. Take time to look really carefully before replacing stones: the longer you look, the more you'll see. Watch out for any movement, shapes or colours that stand out. Listen for crabs clicking and fish flicking the water with their tails.

SLIP 'N' SLDE

'Life is like a slide... So much fun that we get back up every day
and do it again' **LINDA POINDEXTER**

I f the idea of a grown person launching themselves down a man-made slide
sounds idiotic to you, that's because it is... gloriously so. And like many
of the most stupid ideas, a slip 'n' slide is also stupendously fun. Yes, you are
going to score yourself some prize bruises; yes, you are going to look as elegant
as a hippo on ice, but that's the whole point: to make yourself look like a fool
and have a great time doing it.

Our slip 'n' slide was brilliantly easy to make. You simply need some plastic
sheeting, a shovel and some lubricant.

For the sheeting, we used a 10-feet by 100-feet roll of plastic. Your local hardware store, or online retailers, will be able to help. Get the thickest plastic
you can find. If you're doing this at the beach – as we were – then you want
proper protection from rocks and seashells as a tear in the plastic is going to
bring an abrupt end to the fun.

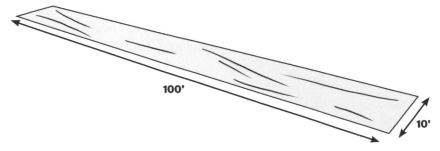

100'

10'

If you are setting up on a lawn or in a park then you'll need to use tent pegs
to secure the sheeting. Be sure to insert them all the way into the ground,
so they don't stick out – for obvious safety reasons.

If you are doing this at the beach, which is probably the best place, then you need a shovel to dig your slide in. It took us about 30 minutes to secure the edges of the plastic sheet by burying them slightly and piling sand along the edge.

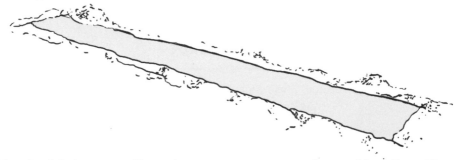

For the lubricant, you'll need a generous amount of something slimy. You can use baby oil, though you'll spend a good deal of time cleaning yourselves off afterwards. We used an environmentally friendly soap (and if you're doing this anywhere near a river or the sea then this is a must). Washing-up liquid is a cheap alternative but again it is environmentally unfriendly and you won't be able to use it in a public place.

Ideally, you will set up your slide somewhere near a hose, so that you can have a steady trickle keeping the slide wet throughout the session. If that's not possible then you'll need a few buckets to add a bit of water after each ride. (Friction is not your friend here.)

BUILDING YOUR SLIP'N'SLIDE
Start by choosing a spot that has a flat space of at least 10 feet by 100 feet, plus roughly 40 feet of 'runway' at one end. Before you begin work, carefully inspect the area to make sure there aren't any stray sharp or hard objects that could damage you or the slide.

Once the area is clear, you can roll out the plastic. As above, bury the edges or use tent pegs to secure in place.

Apply a generous amount of soap or other lubricant along the full length of the slide and then lightly water with your hose or buckets.

You are ready to slide!

As the session goes on, you will need to apply water and more lubricant – generally lubricant need only be added to the top end of the slide and your sliders will then spread it for you as they go.

Be safe:
Don't stand up on the slide
or try to 'surf' it on your feet.
You are asking for trouble.

Only one person at a time. You can get up some serious speed over 100 feet of sliding and collisions can cause nasty accidents.

And remember: if you drink, don't slide!

' ALL GOOD THINGS ARE
WILD AND FREE '

HENRY DAVID THOREAU

PRESS WILD FLOWERS

'Find beauty not only in the thing itself, but in the pattern of the shadows, the light and dark which that thing provides'

JUNICHIRO TANIZAKI

The art of pressing flowers has been practised in Japan since the 16th-century. Known as Oshibana, Samurai warriors practised this delicate art as part of their training, to teach them patience, harmony with nature and concentration. And there is certainly something absorbing and also peaceful about pressing flowers. The skill is to preserve the colours and the structure of each flower as faithfully as possible, so that each remains a snapshot of a moment in time. This requires real skill. And they make a beautiful memento and a thoughtful gift.

There are various methods you can use to press a flower, each with its own advantages, though we chose the two most traditional: making your own press and using a book.

PICK YOUR FLOWERS

Before you begin with the press, you must first select the best flower. Freshness is all.

Choose flowers that are either still in bud form, or which have just bloomed. If you are using a garden, then pluck first thing in the morning, just after the dew.

You want to press flowers right away (if you can't, then you can store them in the fridge in a food bag). There are some important steps to follow to make sure the flowers retain as much colour and freshness as possible:

- First, cut the stems at an angle (as shown).
- Remove any low leaves. If you leave them on then they will rot and shorten the life of the flower.
- Put the flower(s) in a clean vase with water and flower food, or a teaspoon of sugar.
- Keep them somewhere cool and well-ventilated, away from direct sunlight for a few hours.

- Once removed from the vase, split any thick flowers. Flowers with flat faces are easier to press. If you want to press something thick like a rose, for instance, then first use scissors or a knife to halve them.
- Lay them flat on the paper ready for pressing.

THE PAPER

You must dry out your flowers as quickly as possible to stop them from browning. Printer paper is excellent for this, as well as cardboard (not corrugated), facial tissues and coffee filters. Avoid paper towels, as the texture may imprint on the petals.

TO MAKE YOUR OWN WOODEN FLOWER PRESS

Cut two pieces of plywood of 9x12 inch (22.5 cm x 30 cm). Drill holes in the corners of both blocks, making sure that they line up with each other.

Sandwich the flower between two pieces of paper and then insert between the two blocks of wood.

Tighten the blocks together, using wingnuts and bolts.

Once pressed, the flower will need to be held like that for three to four weeks. During that time, you must change the blotting paper roughly every four days, to prevent browning.

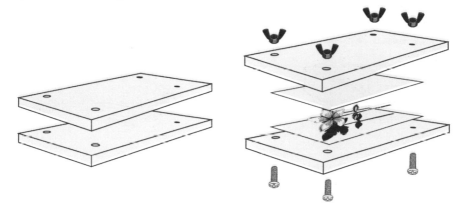

USING A BOOK TO PRESS

This is the most popular way and the easiest. First, pick the heaviest book you can find – a hardback ideally. Bear in mind that the moisture from the flower may cause the pages to wrinkle. So use a book you don't mind being damaged.

Insert the flower between two pieces of paper, as above, and insert them within the pages of the book. You can dry multiple flowers at once, though you'll need to space them throughout the book, so moisture doesn't spread from one flower to another.

Shut the book and use other books, or weights, to weigh it down. Be careful not to disturb the arrangement of the flowers as you shut the book.

Again, you will need to change the blotter sheets every few days.

The flower will be completely dry within 2–3 weeks. Carefully remove it using tweezers or delicate fingers, taking care as it will be extremely delicate.

Pressed flowers look great just about anywhere. You can frame them or if you are feeling more adventurous then they can be used as coasters, phone cases or jewellery.

THE GREAT SCAVENGER HUNT

'We live in a wonderful world that is full of beauty, charm and adventure. There is no end to the adventures that we can have if only we seek them with our eyes open'

JAWAHARLAL NEHRU

S omewhere within us all lies the urge to discover – to head out into the wide world and seek new things. Adult life can draw us into ever-narrowing circles of routine places and objects. The beauty of a scavenger hunt is that it asks us to tap back into that first spirit of discovery.

The idea is very simple: each team is given a list of clues to a series of places and objects that they must find. They do this either by retrieving actual objects and/or simply taking a photo as proof – all against the clock. The first team to collect the clues and return home wins.

You can set up a scavenger hunt anywhere – in a city or in the wildness of the outdoors.

We think the adventure is greater when you are heading out into the great unknown, contesting new ground and encountering the elements. You can also choose whether to go on foot, cycle or by car, but a good old-fashioned yomp on foot seems the best way.

First, players must divide into teams – two teams is all you need but you can have as many as you like depending on the size of your group. Each team must then agree on the rules of travel – i.e. whether cycles, cars and public transport are allowed or you're strictly going by foot.

Players are then handed a clue sheet with a list of specific tasks to complete or specific items to discover.

Players then use a digital camera – or phone – to make a record of each task they complete or place they visit.

You then either agree on a time limit, within which players must complete as many tasks as they can before returning to base, or you simply say that the first team to complete the list wins.

The 'clues' you draw up can range as widely as your imagination (and practicality) allows.

For our hunt we first agreed that players would have to travel by foot – ours took place in a part of the British countryside where public footpaths criss-cross most of the land – and set a time limit of five hours, within which the players would have to discover as many of the clues as possible.

Here are some of the clues we listed:

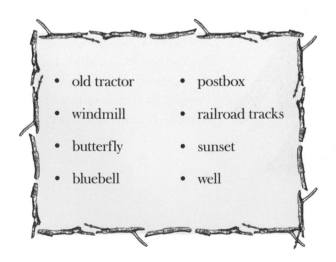

- old tractor
- windmill
- butterfly
- bluebell
- postbox
- railroad tracks
- sunset
- well

Our idea was to mix specific places we knew from the local map (e.g. the windmill) with wildlife, flowers and the sky above that would require the players to constantly have their eyes open to their environment.

A popular alternative is to list tasks as well as places and objects. So, for instance, if you were playing in a town or city you might ask that players help an old person carry their shopping, or take a photo with a man wearing a hat.

You can be as silly as you like or (if you're like us) take it much too seriously and do whatever it takes to win. In either case, it is a fantastic way to immerse yourself in an environment and take notice of things that might otherwise pass you by.

PANNING FOR GOLD

'Men rush to California and Australia as if the true gold were to be found in that direction; but that is to go to the very opposite extreme to where it lies. They go prospecting farther and farther away from the true lead, and are most unfortunate when they think themselves most successful'

HENRY DAVID THOREAU

They called it 'gold fever': the lust that made men leave everything behind to go West and seek their fortune. The California Gold Rush was sparked by the discovery of gold nuggets in the Sacramento Valley in 1848. James Wilson Marshall and John Sutter were two amateur prospectors who chanced upon flakes of gold in a river at the base of the Sierra Nevada mountains in California.

They tried to keep their discovery quiet but news inevitably spread, and in the years that followed thousands of prospective gold miners would flock to the region. 1849 thus became a famous year in US history and the migrants would forever be known as the 49ers. It was a period in which roughly $2 billion worth of gold would be discovered in the region.

Panning for gold was one of the original techniques used, though it was succeeded by hydraulic mining and industrialised methods when the surface gold soon ran out.

You can still pan many rivers around the world today. Your odds of striking it rich are, honestly, not all that great but it's better than playing the lottery and you get to spend a day in the fresh air.

FIND A STREAM OR RIVER WITH GOLD

Perhaps a wisened old prospector clutching a jug of moonshine has told you of a gold-rich river up in the mountains. If not, as ever, the internet is a great resource and should be able to point you in the direction of promising streams and rivers. Do not be put off if a particular place hasn't produced any gold for a long time. Each winter, storms unearth more deposits of gold which will be washed downstream as small flakes and nuggets, so each year brings new opportunity.

PICK YOUR SPOT

You want somewhere along the side of a stream or river where the water is a minimum 6 inches deep. Any shallower than that and the water could be too full of mud and debris for you to see clearly.

The water needs to be moving fast enough for it to wash the silt and debris from your pan, but slow enough so that it doesn't disturb your panning motions when your pan is submerged.

Try to find somewhere comfortable to sit, such as a fallen log or a large rock. Panning requires patience, and your body will be grateful for the relief.

CHOOSE YOUR PAN

Most pans are made of either plastic or metal. Plastic is better for beginners because it is lighter, doesn't rust, is black-coloured (which makes it easier to spot any gold), and often they are ribbed to catch the gold.

Or, you can be a true 49er and use an old-school metal pan for the sake of authenticity if nothing else.

HOW TO PAN

Using a shovel, take a good amount of soil from the river's edge and tip it into your pan to fill it up to about three-quarters full.

Submerge the pan at the water's edge, so it is just beneath the surface. Now, shake the pan vigorously several times – first back and forth and then side to side. You want some water to enter the pan as you shake but do not shake it so hard that the materials get washed clean out of the pan.

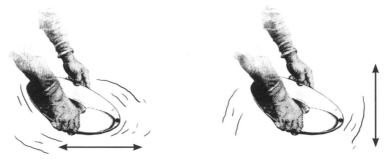

Stop shaking and switch to a gentler, circular motion. You want the gravel to begin spinning within the pan. This should make most of the dirt and clay wash from the pan or dissolve.

Pick out the larger rocks, making sure that they are washed clean and you aren't missing anything, and repeat these steps until all the large rocks are gone and the heavier concentrates (which may include gold as well as sand) have settled at the bottom of the pan.

You next need to wash out the lighter sand and gravel. To do so, tilt the pan slightly away from you as if you are trying to catch the current of water. Swirl the pan from side to side, with a forward tossing motion. Again you need to be careful not to lose the contents of the pan but you want to do it with enough force to spill the lighter gravel at the top of the pan out over the edge.

Now, level the pan again and, keeping it in the water, use a back and forward shaking motion. This will cause the gold to settle at the bottom of the pan and the lighter material to rise to the surface.

Repeat this process until there are only about two cups of heavier material left in the pan, which should be made up of 'black sand' – i.e. concentrates – and hopefully some gold.

To wash out the black sand, remove your pan from the water but first make sure there is roughly an inch of water left inside – you will need this to continue to sift the sand from the gold.

Tilt the pan towards you and slowly swirl the contents in a circle. This will allow you to check whether there are any large pieces of gold that can be picked by hand.

Keep doing this until you can't tell any more gold apart from the black sand. Another advantage to using a plastic pan is that you can use a magnet to separate sand from gold.

Collect your gold in a bottle, taking special care and using a funnel.

Head into town for a night of wild celebration!

WATER-BALLOON DODGEBALL

'Only those who are capable of silliness can truly be called intelligent'
CHRISTOPHER ISHERWOOD

What better way to enjoy yourself on a scorching-hot summer's day than hurling balloons full of ice-cold water? Playing this game, we were instantly transported back to baking-hot childhood summers spent in the garden. And by combining water-balloons with the supremely fun game of dodgeball, you are guaranteed enough competition to keep things interesting.

You will need a good number of balloons. We played 3 vs 3 and got through about 100 balloons. (And if you're like us you'll quickly discover that far more burst from hitting ground rather than body shots.) The more people you have on hand to help, the less time you'll have to spend on prep.

Look for medium-sized balloons that won't burst too easily. Fill them up (from a tap is easiest) and tie them off.

Divide your group into two teams (play with uneven teams if you have to – if ever there was a sport that was too silly for people to have to sit out, this is it).

The best way to begin the game is what's called an 'opening rush' whereby you place three balloons in the centre of the field ('the dead zone') and three players from each team must race from the backline of the court to retrieve them. Players must return to their back court area before any balloons can be thrown.

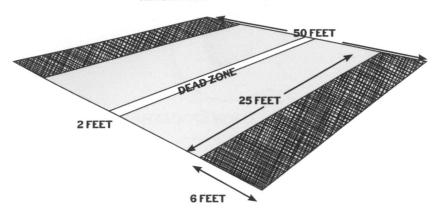

50 FEET

DEAD ZONE

25 FEET

2 FEET

6 FEET

An official dodgeball court is roughly 50 feet by 25 feet but you'll want to just play within a decent area, depending on where you are.

The rules of dodgeball are that each player is 'out' when they are hit with a ball. You can choose in this water-balloon version whether getting hit is enough, or the balloon actually needs to burst on impact for it to count. (It depends partly how fragile or not your balloons are.) You can also eliminate a player by catching their thrown balloon – only if it doesn't burst. If that happens, you also bring one of your 'out' players back into the game.

A game is won either when all of the opposing team have been eliminated, or if you have more players than the opposing team at the end of a two-minute match.

Headshots are not allowed in proper dodgeball – and that's probably a good rule to carry over to the water-balloon version as it can still sting.

WALKING MEDITATION

'When we pay attention to nature's music, we find that everything on the earth contributes to its harmony' **HAZRAT INAYAT KHAN**

There has been a recent surge of interest in mindfulness and other forms of meditation. Maybe this is a response to the increasingly frantic and fast-paced nature of modern life that seems to draw our attention in a million directions at once. At its core, meditation teaches us the habit of focusing the mind and body; to quiet our thoughts and truly notice what is going on around us as well as within our bodies and mind.

The outdoors provide the perfect space in which to engage in meditation and by walking, and putting our bodies in motion, we set a rhythm for our minds to latch on to. And the space through which we walk, whether the scenery is composed of birds and trees or cars and lampposts, offers the perfect focus for our thoughts.

In walking meditation, the idea is to use the experience of walking as your focus. The fundamental difference from other forms of meditation is that you keep your eyes open throughout (unless you want to walk straight into a tree). As such, the idea is not to withdraw your attention from the outside world to the same extent as you would when practising mindful breathing, for instance.

Instead, you must remain aware of things outside yourself – the wind, the sun, the rain, as well as the sounds of birds, cars or whatever you can hear.

One of the great advantages of walking meditation is that it can be easier for many people to be aware of their body while moving than it is to sit and meditate. And, of course, it is a practice that can be worked into your daily life, as you travel from place to place.

Walking meditation is what's known as a 'meditation in action' and the idea is to use the physical, mental and emotional experiences of walking to develop greater awareness. This is a way of defragmenting our minds – putting them back together to make a whole. To be more whole is to be more contented and fulfilled.

HOW TO BEGIN

Standing – the meditation begins by simply standing on the spot. As you stand, be aware of your weight being transferred through the soles of your feet, down into the earth. Be aware of the subtle movements and constant adjustments going on in order to keep you balanced and staying upright.

Once you have that awareness, you can begin to walk. Start at a slowish pace and walk in your normal way. You're not going to be doing anything physically different during this meditation, only being more aware of it.

As you walk, start by keeping your attention on the soles of your feet and the alternating pattern of contact and release with the floor. Be aware of the fact that your heel first touches down and then rolls forward on to the ball before lifting and moving through the air. Notice all the various sensations in your feet – the way your toes touch against each other, the feeling of the inside of your shows, the way your socks' material feels. Let your feet be as relaxed as possible. Become aware of your ankles. Notice the sensations in your joints.

Next, let this awareness of your body move upwards, noticing first your calves at each stage of their movement, then your knee joints, thigh muscles, hips, pelvis, belly, chest, shoulders, arms, wrists, hands – keep noticing every detail of the experience and how the different parts of your body are connected.

Become aware of your neck, the muscles holding up your head, and how different movements affect the way you feel. When you put your chin on your chest, for instance, you may notice that your experience becomes more introspective and emotional, whereas when you lift your chin your experience might be lighter and drawn by all the passing things that you notice.

Relax your jaw and relax your eyes. Let your eyes be gently focused, looking ahead. You are not staring at anything and not allowing yourself to get caught up in anything that is passing in front of you.

YOUR FEELINGS

You can begin to be aware of your feelings. Notice whether there are things that are pleasant or unpleasant in or outside of your body. Just notice them, don't cling on or push them away. Let them drift by without either pursuing them or averting your gaze.

YOUR THOUGHTS AND EMOTIONS

Notice your emotional state. Are you happy? Bored? Annoyed? Notice your mind too. Is it clear? Calm? Busy? Do not judge, only notice. In practising mindfulness, you are trying to be more aware of how your experience moves from sensation, to feeling, to emotion, so that you have more choice over what emotions you experience.

See if you can find a point of balance; where you are equally aware of what's going on outside you and within, so your mind is quiet and calm.

Next, you must stop. Not so that you suddenly come to a halt but so you bring your walk to a gradual end. Just experience yourself standing again and notice what it's like to not be moving, focusing once more on the weight travelling down through you and the complex act of keeping yourself upright before finally bringing this session of meditation to a stop.

Notice the world around you and try to hold that balance between your awareness of the inner and outer worlds.

Many people experience an increase in their physical sensitivity as well as a sense of joy, happiness and even bliss.

Before you move on with your day, give yourself a bit of time to assimilate the effects of the meditation. Try to maintain some of this state of balance and as much as possible carry this meditative attitude forwards with you in the rest of your day. With practice, walking meditation will help you to feel more attentive, patient and calm.

Build a Campfire

'[When] you've lost all your dreams,
there's nothin' like a campfire and a can of beans'

TOM WAITS

Human inventions do not come much older or more significant than the humble campfire. Recent evidence suggests that Homo erectus was huddling around a blazing fire, making antelope burgers, some 1.6 million years ago.

Indeed, the ability to control fire in this way was a pivotal moment in the evolution of our species.

Campfires first enabled our ancestors to survive the bitterly cold nights and thus to migrate into colder territories. They also warned off predators, meaning we could spend less time hiding in the trees and remain on the ground doing important things like learning to walk. And they allowed us to cook meat (which ultimately made our brains bigger), as well as making our weapons more deadly.

In the story of humankind, then, the campfire must have a starring role. Fundamental as it is, though, fire-making is nonetheless a skill which many of us don't have. Should you find yourself out in the wilds at night, you would do well to know these basics.

CREATING A FIRE BED
When dealing with fire, safety must always come first. If the campsite or park you are in has a designated fire area then use it.

If not, be sure to pick a site away from trees, bushes and any other vegetation. Your fire bed must be on bare earth and not grass. If you can't find a bare place, then you need to dig and rake away plant material. Your bed must be made from a dirt platform roughly 3–4 inches thick.

GATHERING WOOD

A campfire is made of three basic components: tinder, kindling and fuel wood. When looking for wood, always look to see that it snaps or breaks easily. If it bends then it is too wet. And collect twice as much as you expect you will need – you will burn through it much more quickly than you think.

Tinder: This is the beginning of every good campfire. Tinder catches easily but burns quickly. Dry leaves and bark, wood shavings and dry grass all work well.

Kindling: With your tinder aflame, you can't move directly to logs of wood as they will smother the flame. Kindling is usually made from small twigs and branches about the width of a pencil. (Like tinder, it will need to be dry or it won't catch.) If your kindling is wet then you can try using a knife to whittle away the damp bark.

Fuel wood: This is what will keep your fire burning. It doesn't have to be huge logs. You want to find branches that are roughly the width of your wrist.

STARTING A FIRE

Short of having a box of matches – which should form part of any outdoor kit – there are various ingenious ways that you can start a fire. You can use a lens to focus the sun's rays, you can use a battery to light some steel wool, you can carry a flint and steel set which will quickly generate a shower of sparks. In truth, any of these methods and various others would be easier to pull off than the 'friction method' we associate with true survival situations – think Tom Hanks in Castaway.

However, if you are truly stranded in the middle of nowhere, with only the environment to hand, then you are most likely going to need to call on some form of the friction method.

Friction-based fire-making is not for those who give up easily, to put it mildly. That is to say, it's incredibly frustrating and will likely take you lots and lots of attempts before you succeed. There are various methods you can use but all of them apply the same principle of spinning a stick, or 'spindle', on a fireboard and using the resulting friction to create an ember that will start your fire.

Perhaps the most important aspect of the friction method is the type of wood that you use for the fireboard and spindle. Aspen, juniper, willow, cedar, cypress and walnut are ideal and, as ever with fire-making, you want them to be bone dry.

The simplest and most effective form of the friction method is the bow drill. The bowing will make it easier to keep up the speed and pressure you need to create enough friction. As well as a spindle and fireboard, you will need a socket and bow.

Have your nest of tinder ready to one side. You can make this out of anything that catches fire easily, such as dry grass, leaves and bark. Once you create an ember, you will need to quickly insert it into the nest.

BOW AND DRILL

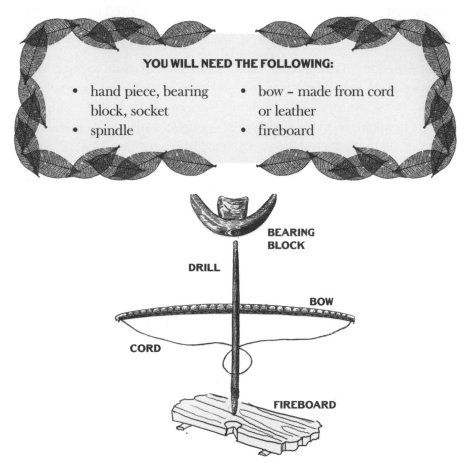

The bearing block holds the top end of the spindle in place while it rotates. You want it to be as smooth as possible, so the friction is directed to the fireboard. It can be made of bone, sea shells, stone or steel. However, you are most likely to take a piece of hard wood and make an indent using your knife into which the top end of the spindle can be placed.

The spindle is made from a piece of hardwood and should be eight to sixteen inches in length and half an inch in diameter. Use your knife to sharpen one end to a dull point. This sharpened end goes into the bearing block.

The fireboard should be roughly an inch thick. Look for wood from fallen trees that are not touching the ground. This helps to slow the wood decay while allowing it to slowly dry (freshly cut wood is very moist).

To prepare the board for drilling, first place the spindle's end about half an inch from the back edge of the fireboard and mark the point. Use your knife to create a small nook for the spindle and drill for 30 seconds to clearly mark the diameter of the spindle on the board.

In order for the wood dust created by the drilling to shape into a coal, you need to cut a notch in the fireboard. Cut a 'v' shape in the side of the fireboard, so it intersects with the spindle's drilling mark

Use bark from the same tree as before to catch the ember as you are drilling. (This is known as an ember pan.) This keeps the ember off the cold, damp ground.

The bow should be made of flexible wood, such as willow. We used parachute cord as our string but you could use shoe laces, strips of leather and even vines.

Attach the cord to the bow and twist the spindle into the bow string.

Hold the bearing block in one hand and the bow in the other. Place one foot on the fireboard. Support your arm with the bearing block against your shin and point the bow slightly downward and begin to drill at a steady pace. Once the board starts to smoke, speed up. Do not stop!

The 'v' notch allows wood dust to drop down and create a hot coal. Tap the hearth board with your knife to help separate the coal from the board. You don't want to break it into pieces.

Place the coal in the middle of the tinder nest and blow on it until the tinder catches.

LAY THE FIRE

There are three common ways to lay a fire:

TEEPEE FIRE LAY

Place your tinder in a pile in the middle of your campfire site. On top of this bundle, set a tepee with kindling. Leave an opening in the tepee on the side from which the wind is blowing – this will ensure your fire gets the air it needs.

Continue to add kindling to the tepee, each piece larger than the last until you reach pencil-sized twigs.

Around this, create a larger tepee structure with the fuel wood.

Next, place a match (or your coal) under the tinder. The flame should naturally rise to the kindling and then the fuel wood.

Eventually the tepee will collapse, at which point you pile on the fuel logs

LEAN-TO FIRE LAY

Stick a long piece of kindling into the ground at a 30 degree angle, with the end facing into the wind.

Place a tinder bundle beneath the support stick.

Surround this bundle of tinder with small pieces of kindling.

Lay small pieces of kindling against the piece stuck into the ground. Add another layer using larger pieces of kindling.

Light the tinder and watch the whole thing burn.

LOG CABIN FIRE LAY

This lay begins with a small tepee lay.

Lay large pieces of fuel wood on the opposite side of the tepee.

Next, lay some smaller pieces of fuel wood across the first set of fuel wood, parallel on the other side of the tepee.

Repeat the pattern, laying smaller and shorter pieces to form a pyramid shape, as shown, before lighting.

PUTTING OUT YOUR CAMPFIRE

It is essential that when you are finished with your fire you make sure it is properly extinguished.

This can take longer than you think, so give yourself a good 30 minutes before you need to leave or go to bed.

With a bucketful of water, sprinkle as much as you need to put out the embers and charcoal. As you sprinkle, stir the embers with a stick, ensuring that all the ashes get wet until you can no longer see steam or hear hissing noises.

Put the back of your hand near (but not on!) the ashes. If you still feel heat, it's too hot to leave. Keep adding water and stirring. Once it feels cool, you are all set.

Scoop the ashes into a bag and spread them around the campsite, before replacing the dirt from the fire bed.

KEEPING ANIMALS AWAY FROM YOUR CAMPSITE

'There are no wild animals unless man makes them so'

MARK TWAIN

KEEPING ANIMALS AWAY FROM YOUR CAMPSITE

When we spend time in the wild, we share an environment with countless living things. It is essential not only to be respectful of this surrounding wild-life but also to take the necessary precautions to protect yourself and your fellow campers from unwanted intruders. In an extreme case that might mean repelling an 800-pound grizzly bear (although bears typically don't attack unless threatened). If you are camping in the UK or somewhere similar, then you won't have to worry about bears.

The brown bear went extinct from Britain around AD 1000. Nor will you need to be concerned about wolves, which haven't been seen since the late 17th-century.

You might just stumble across a wild boar, however: a poten-tially dangerous animal which has been reintroduced in recent years in the name of good sausages. And more usu-ally the night-time brings with it a host of unwanted pests hoping to crawl into your tents or campsite, such as raccoons, mice and squirrels.

HERE ARE FEW TIPS TO KEEPING ANIMALS AWAY

- Keep all foods inside coolers or containers with lockable lids wherever possible. To be double safe, you can secure it with a rope (see 'knots you must know'). Use rope to hang the cooler from a tree limb, seven feet from the ground.
- Always eat outside and do not store food in the tent. Snacks should never be kept inside and nor should your toothpaste – the peppermint smell quickly attracts lots of animals, including bears.
- Similarly, if you are catching, killing and preparing animals (including fish) then do it either at the water's edge or well away from the camp.
- Wash pots, pans and dishes thoroughly after use. Mice in particular are drawn to dirty utensils left lying around in campsites and can leave nasty germs. More perilously, they can also leave seriously toxic faeces which can make you very ill.
- A great tip is to bring along sheets and pillows that have been soaked in fabric softener. Animals do not like the smell and will keep their distance, and it will also help to mask any food smells that might be coming from the campsite.
- Most animals are afraid of fire – yet another reason why it represents one of mankind's greatest ever inventions. A campfire will help deter most unwanted attentions. (Beware, though, it is a myth that lions are afraid of fire. In fact, they are often drawn to investigate it.)
- Making noise is another way to keep animals from intruding. You can leave a battery-operated radio playing at low volume while you sleep.
- Keep your garbage well away from the campsite, as this will attract animals.
- Lastly, some outdoorsmen recommend urinating close to the camp perimeter to help warn off intruders. You will have to weigh up that possible benefit versus the faint smell of urine on the breeze.

THE ONLY KNOT YOU NEED TO KNOW

'When you reach the end of your rope, tie a knot in it and hang on'
THOMAS JEFFERSON

The art of tying a knot is a subject of almost limitless scope. The seminal work on the subject, *The Ashley Book of Knots*, weighs in at a whopping 3,800 entries. So, to claim that any single knot is the only one you need to know is pretty hard to back up.

However, *The Ashley Book* was the culmination of more than 11 years of work. The book in your hands is about getting out into the wild. And so often in an outdoor environment it is your ability to make do and adapt to a given situation that saves the day.

With that in mind, the genius of the bowline knot is its versatility. Whether you are strapping something to the roof of your car, hanging a food container from a tree, or simply joining two things together, the bowline offers a reliable solution.

Begin by making a loop by crossing the 'free' part of the line (i.e. the bit nearest the end of the rope) over the top.

Bring the end of the line up through the hole.

Take the end around the 'standing' part of the line.

Put the end back through the hole.

Finally, pull both ends to tighten the knot.

When learning, use a length of rope about 3 feet long.

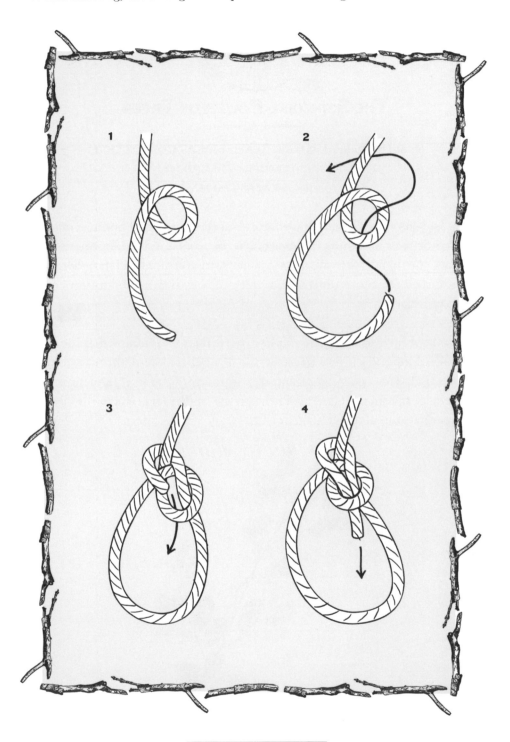

THE SPIRITUAL POWER OF TREES

'I said to the almond tree, "Friend, speak to me of God,"
and the almond tree blossomed'

NIKOS KAZANTZAKIS

Okay, cue eye-rolling. Many will consider the very idea of 'spiritual energy' ridiculous and think tree-hugging is the worst kind of hippy nonsense. On the other hand, there are several major world religions still in rude health so perturbed by nature worship they deem it a sin worthy of punishment by death or worse.

Without wishing to antagonise either party, the fact remains that the worship of nature and of trees in particular is a belief system almost as old as humankind. Trees play significant roles in many of the world's mythologies and religions, from the Garden of Eden to the Bodhi Tree, where Buddha sat and meditated to attain enlightenment.

Druids and pagans practised their worship among sacred groves, and in parts of India there are acknowledged holy trees to this day.

Even those of us who don't believe in spirituality as such might have sensed a specialness and unique elemental power in trees. They provide the planet with oxygen, give shelter and life to the animal kingdom and supply us with chemicals essential to modern medicine. And a walk in the woods, or time spent sitting in the shade of a tree can bring on a profound calmness.

Is it truly possible, though, that trees are giving out something more intangible? Well, for those who believe in such things, trees like all living things have an energy frequency and an aura. Because trees have roots reaching deep underground, they have strong 'grounding energy' and as such have a slower, deeper, more concentrated vibration than other living things. If you believe that then you might also conclude that by coming into contact with a tree you can pick up on these vibrations and in doing so become more centred and grounded. Perhaps this is why we often feel comforted and secure in the presence of trees.

This is the basis of the infamous tree-hugging, which has – sadly perhaps – become a negative term for hippy behaviour.

However, if you can swallow your cynicism and are curious to try it, then why not hug a tree?

Here's how:

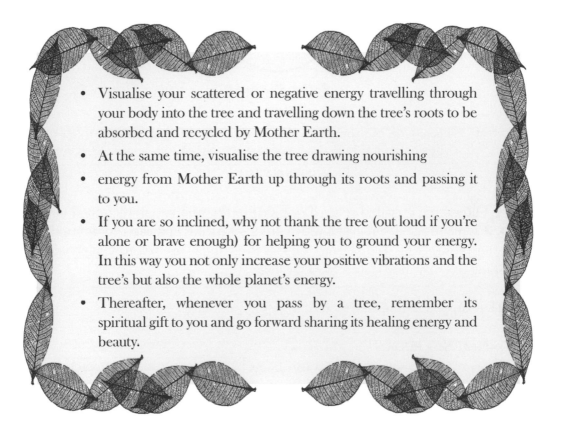

- Visualise your scattered or negative energy travelling through your body into the tree and travelling down the tree's roots to be absorbed and recycled by Mother Earth.
- At the same time, visualise the tree drawing nourishing
- energy from Mother Earth up through its roots and passing it to you.
- If you are so inclined, why not thank the tree (out loud if you're alone or brave enough) for helping you to ground your energy. In this way you not only increase your positive vibrations and the tree's but also the whole planet's energy.
- Thereafter, whenever you pass by a tree, remember its spiritual gift to you and go forward sharing its healing energy and beauty.

Whether you believe the tree gifted you its spiritual power, or you don't buy a word of it and simply felt you had a calming, meditative experience in your mind, ultimately, perhaps, it doesn't matter which it was...

DIY FISHING

'The charm of fishing is that it is the pursuit of what is elusive
but attainable, a perpetual series of occasions for hope'

JOHN BUCHAN

S hould you ever find yourself stranded in the wild and in the mood for
some sushi, or simply out with a group of friends and eager to show off
your prowess as a wild person, you can easily improvise fishing equipment
using everyday things and a bit of ingenuity.

Here are seven simple methods

IMPROVISE A HOOK
First, you need something that can be fashioned into a hook. Paperclips,
ring-pulls, sharp twigs and bobby pins are all good candidates.

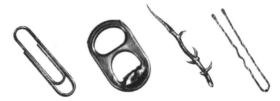

Next, you need to add a line to the hook. If you don't have any string to hand,
then shoelaces, threads of clothing and even long blades of grass will work.

To bait the hook you can use any scraps of food
you might have or dead insects that you can gather.
Failing that, some colourful bits of plastic, leaves
or jewellery will do the trick.

Dangle the hook in a shadowy area, such as beneath an overhanging bank, line of trees or near rocks.

Once you have a fish on the line, do not attempt to haul it in on the line as it will break. Instead, use your hands or some kind of net made of clothing.

CORNERING THE FISH
This is easier done as a team rather than solo.

First, you will need something to block the fish's route and corral it, such as a length of cloth. Holding one end in the water, while your partner holds the other, make sure there is no room beneath for the fish to escape.

Move slowly towards the fish and corral them towards an area from which they can't escape, e.g. a bend in the river or the end of a tidepool.

Once the fish are backed into a small enough area, scoop them up with your container, as below.

COLLECTING BY HAND
This technique requires the most skill and patience. First, you need to find a hideout – it is best done in shallow water, either a low tide, or a shallow river or stream.

Slowly lower your hand into the water and into the hideout, with your palm facing upward and fingers extended towards the fish.

DIY FISHING

Keep your hand as still as possible, so as not to alarm the fish, and then very gradually inch towards it.

You need to approach until you can feel the fish's chin, at which point you close your fingers around its gills and pull it from the water in one quick snapping motion.

USING A TRAP

Improvise a trap container from clothing, a bucket, jar, plastic container or shopping bag.

Lay the trap in a shadowy area, as above, and wait for a fish to enter. Be poised to quickly pull up the container when the time comes.

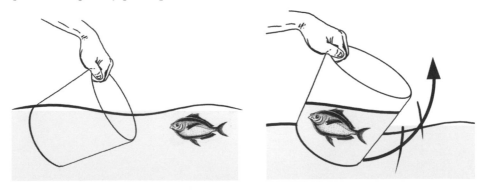

BAILING OUT

This method is still practised regularly in parts of Africa and southern Asia. Find a small area of water – either a pond, or tidal pool, etc. Using a container, bail water from the pool.

Once you have removed enough water and the fish are easily accessible, use your container to scoop them up.

USING WAX

Take a ball or piece of wax (the more colourful, the better) and thread through something strong – either a piece of string or a shoelace.

Tie the string securely to a strong branch and dangle the wax in the water.

Wait for a fish to bite, then pull up the string.

MAKE A SPEARING DEVICE

Useful items you can use to improvise here are pocket knives, scrap pieces of metal, glass or hard plastic and scissor blades.

Alternatively you can simply sharpen a stick to a fine point.

To use this method, fasten your sharp item to a stick using twine, shoelaces or a thread of clothing.

You will need to adjust for refraction in the water. The fish will seem closer than they actually are, so practise stabbing your spear to get a feel for how much you have to adjust your aim.

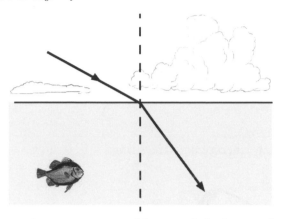

You only get one chance to spear a fish, so wait for it to settle within a reasonably small area.

Aim and stab as quickly and explosively as possible.

SPLITTING LOGS

'The wood warmed me twice, once while I was splitting them, and again
when they were on the fire, so that no fuel could give out more heat'

HENRY DAVID THOREAU

Thoreau was not alone in his praise of splitting wood. Great figures from history including Leo Tolstoy and George Bernard Shaw found in this humble
act a way of not only invigorating the body but also the mind. Trees are the
sentinels of the wild – the oldest and most mysterious creatures of what was
once a prehistoric world. And when we engage in their care (as responsible
tree-work, or the 'coppice'), we become a part of that living history.

Whereas to chop wood you might use an axe, for the job of splitting you will
need a maul. This is essentially a thicker, more 'wedge-shaped' axe, with a
blunt sledgehammer edge on the back of the blade. A maul is typically several
pounds heavier than an axe, which makes the job of splitting the wood easier.

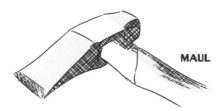

MAUL

First, you will need wood that has been cut to the right length. If you are
handy with a chainsaw then great, but otherwise you are going to want to buy
it pre-cut. Most stoves and fireplaces are designed for a 16–20 inch (40–50 cm)
log and as a rule, the shorter the log, the easier it will be to split.

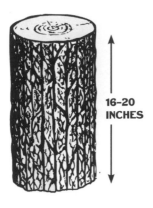

16–20
INCHES

If you are cutting your own wood then be sure to cut it square and flat, as each piece will need to be stood securely on end to be split.

Prepare a chopping block. This is usually a broad section taken from the tree's trunk. It will form the surface on which your logs are to be split. By setting up this surface roughly 16 inches above the ground, you are lessening the strain on your back and reducing the risk of the maul ricocheting and causing real damage.

Always split on some kind of block and never on the ground or a hard floor like concrete.

Set up somewhere safe – you will need a good footing and to avoid any overhanging limbs that could interfere with your work.

Be sure to wear protective gear, including good-quality gloves to protect you from splinters, safety glasses and work boots (ideally with a steel toe).

Never split wood alone – make sure you have someone with you in case of an accident.

HOW TO SPLIT WOOD

Place a log on the chopping block, making sure that it is stable and positioned near the centre of the block. (An unsteady block of wood can be incredibly dangerous, as a glancing blow of the maul could strike your leg or send a projectile of wood flying, so be sure it is steady before you begin.)

First, examine the wood. Look for any hairline cracks - if there are any then aim so that the blade runs in the same direction as the crack.

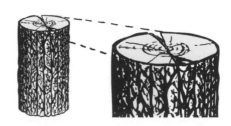

Different woods split differently – for instance, oak splits best through its centre whereas maple splits more easily towards the edges of the end grain. Do some online research once you know which type of wood you are working with.

Aim well. Set your feet square, choose where you want to split the log, and rest your maul on that spot. You may want to make a small indentation into the wood to give you a visual mark at which to aim.

You don't 'swing' a maul and you don't need to draw the end behind your head at any point. Instead, hold the maul firmly with your non-writing hand at the end of the handle and cradle the maul just below its head with your dominant hand.

Bend your knees slightly, then lift the maul straight up above your head, extending your arms straight.

Now slide your dominant hand down the maul until your hands are close. Then bring your hands down and flick your wrists, letting gravity do as much work as possible.

Technique is everything and power is unnecessary. Wild swinging is dangerous and won't split the wood properly.

If the wood hasn't split with the first strike, then you will need to pull and twist the maul firmly to remove it. If it's stuck, then try rocking the axe bit up and down to work it free from the wood.

Repeat your striking action until the wood splits. Try to strike in the exact same spot as the first time, or along the length of any cracks which have appeared.

6-8 INCHES

HOW TO SPLIT WITH A WEDGE

Hardwoods that are gnarled, crooked or are especially knotty can present a challenge for the humble maul. In this case, a steel wedge can help you to overcome even the most stubborn of logs.

First, find a crack in the wood and set the wedge in it so that it sits as firmly as possible.

Use a large hammer or, taking great care, the edge of the maul to tap the wedge further into the wood (as you would drive a nail).

Once the wedge is set firmly in the crack, you are ready to use the maul. Taking great care to be accurate, swing the maul with one firm action so that it lands a blow on top of the wedge. As the wedge is driven into the wood, it will prise the two sides of the crack open.

Continue to do this until the wedge is driven to the point where it splits the log in two. If the wedge has been buried into the wood and the log still isn't split, then you may need to place a second wedge in the crack, further along.

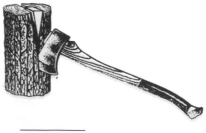

STACKING WOOD

'From the little spark may burst a mighty flame'

DANTE

Although it might not be immediately obvious, there is very much a right way and a wrong way to stack firewood. If you want your hard-earned pile to burn properly when the time comes, then you will need to make sure it is first correctly stacked.

In order for firewood to burn freely, it must first be properly seasoned. This does not mean, sadly, applying salt and pepper to taste but instead allowing it to dry so that the moisture content is as near as possible to 20 per cent. Any more moisture than that and the wood will struggle to catch light, will require far more attention to keep it burning properly and will create an undesirable amount of smoke.

There is also the risk that any firewood not correctly stored will develop mould and mildew that will prevent it from being safely burned inside the home.

All of the above can be avoided with a well-constructed stack. And, aside from the practical benefits, stacking wood can be a calming, quietly joyful experience. Watching a well-prepared log glow in the hearth and warm your home is one of life's great satisfactions.

SELECTING A LOCATION

The first step is to find the right place in which to build your stack. Since stacks can attract termites and other wood-loving creatures, make sure to build it well away from the foundations of your house and any other structures. You also need to bear in mind any drainage issues, to keep moisture away from your stack. So, if your land is on a slope be sure to build at the top end, to stop rainwater and snowfall from draining into the stack. Lastly, choose a spot that gets as much sunshine as possible. This will speed up the drying process.

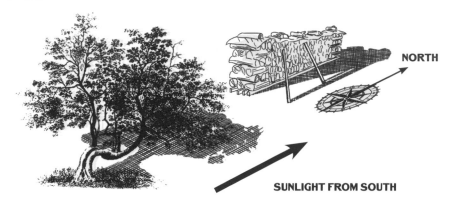

Lay out eight long lengths of pressure-treated 2x4s. These will form the base of your stack, and provide a platform to keep the logs from touching the ground.

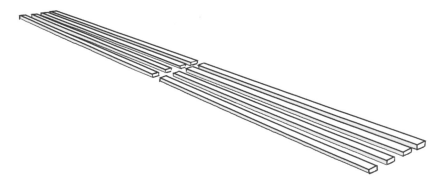

CREATING TOWERS TO SECURE THE STACK

Like books on a shelf, your firewood stack needs to be held in place at both ends to stop it from toppling. This can be done with several pieces of evenly sized firewood.

STACKING WOOD

Start by laying three pieces parallel to each other. Then, place three more pieces on top, laying perpendicular to the original logs. Repeat this pattern until the stack has reached at least six layers high.

This tower will form one book end of your firewood stack. Repeat this process several feet away in order to make the other book end.

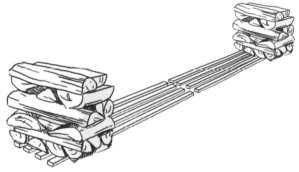

STACKING THE FIREWOOD

Now that you are ready to begin stacking the firewood, the first thing you need to do is work out which direction is west. Most of the wood's moisture will be expelled through the cut ends and since prevailing winds tend to travel east to west, you want the cut ends to be facing in this direction, rather than north to south.

Once you know which direction you are going to be stacking, begin by laying firewood in an irregular pattern. You want to alternate the sizes and shapes of the logs, so that air is able to circulate between each. You also want to place each log a small distance apart to help with quicker drying.

AIR FLOW

Continue doing this until your stack reaches the same height as the towers. If you have any firewood left over then you will need to begin a new stack. (Don't simply chuck it on top of the existing pile as it will interfere with the air flow and could topple the whole thing.)

Be sure to stack firewood together according to when it was cut. This way, you will always know which wood is ready to burn and which needs more seasoning.

It can take up to eight months for the wood to dry.

STACKING WOOD

BUILD A RAFT

'We said there warn't no home like a raft, after all. Other places do seem so cramped up and smothery, but a raft don't. You feel mighty free and easy and comfortable on a raft'

THE ADVENTURES OF HUCKLEBERRY FINN

For any people familiar with Mark Twain's great adventure story, the humble log raft is an immediate and powerful symbol of a free life. There is romance in the idea of being carried aboard your own private vessel, going only where the river takes you and never knowing what lies around the next bend.

If you want to be totally authentic to that vision then you can build a raft using just logs and twine, but we found that in reality this was barely able to support one person and was no good for a journey covering any proper distance.

The raft described below is still simple to make but sturdy enough to ferry you on your journey of adventure.

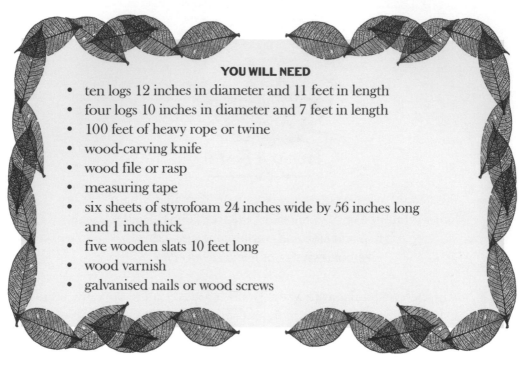

- ten logs 12 inches in diameter and 11 feet in length
- four logs 10 inches in diameter and 7 feet in length
- 100 feet of heavy rope or twine
- wood-carving knife
- wood file or rasp
- measuring tape
- six sheets of styrofoam 24 inches wide by 56 inches long and 1 inch thick
- five wooden slats 10 feet long
- wood varnish
- galvanised nails or wood screws

If you are building your raft in a wooded area then you may be able to source some of these materials from fallen trees – poplar, spruce and cottonwood are the best for raft-building as opposed to heavier woods such as oak. You may also be able to get hold of the Styrofoam from a recycling plant. The other materials can be ordered online or sourced from your local hardware shop.

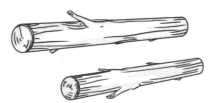

Once you have all the items you need, take the tape measure and mark out a distance of ten feet on the floor. Place one of the shorter logs at each end. These logs will support the main deck and ensure the front and rear of the raft remain in place.

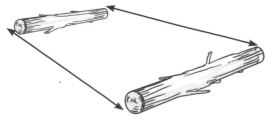

You need to flatten the tops of these shorter logs, so that the longer logs which are to be placed on top won't roll off. You can do this using the wood rasp (effectively a large file) to shave their tops, or alternatively using a knife, taking great care.

Next, lay the longer logs on top, so that they are in the opposite direction to the shorter logs. (You can shave the bottom of the longer logs too, if you find that they are still rolling about too much.)

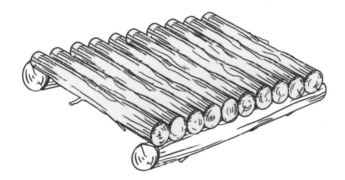

Take the remaining short logs and shave their tops too. They then need to be placed flat-side down on the longer logs, directly above where the other two shorts logs are placed. This sandwiches the main deck between the four support logs, to keep the whole raft held together.

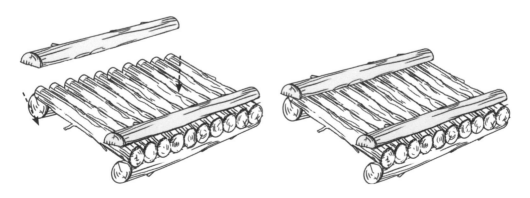

Use the rope or twine (if you're really wild, you can try using some vines) to tie the support logs together. Once they are tied in place, lash the deck logs to the support logs. Be sure to criss-cross the rope as you wrap it around each log and pull it as tight as you can to stop the logs from moving about.

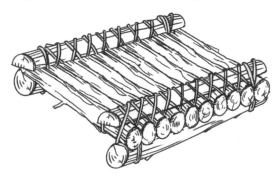

With your deck secured, you can flip the whole thing over to add the flotation. The Styrofoam sheets must be placed between the support logs.

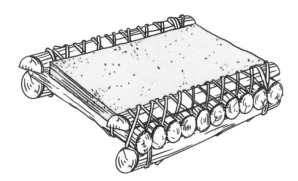

Then the wooden slats are placed on top of the Styrofoam and nailed to the support logs. The flotation is now secured in place.

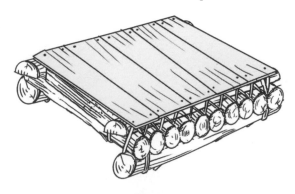

BUILD A RAFT

Finally, you need to varnish the entire thing. This will stop the wood from absorbing water and rotting. You need between three to five layers of varnish, letting the raft dry between each coat.

To steer the boat you need only a good long stick to act as a pole.

Before you set off, check with the local authority that you are allowed to raft on your chosen body of water. ALWAYS wear a life jacket and try to wear clothes that are waterproof or which will dry quickly.

WILDFLOWERS

'There are always flowers, for those who want to see them'

HENRI MATISSE

Simply put, a 'wildflower' is any species which grows without need of human hand. Some species are indigenous to their continent, and known as 'natives', while others that have been introduced from other parts of the world are 'naturalised'.

The common feature of both is that they are able to grow on their own in nature and to our mind this lends wildflowers a special kind of beauty. Added to that, most wild flowers are beautiful, colourful and fragrant.

In order to find wild flowers, explore your local wild places. Use online resources (e.g. the US Forest Service or the National Trust) to discover the best spots, as well as the rules as to what you are and are not allowed to take home with you.

VARIOUS VARIETIES OF WORT

TO PICK OR NOT TO PICK

In the UK, it is usually not an offence to pick the 'Four Fs' – fruit, foliage, fungi or flowers – if the plants are growing wild and it is for your personal use and not for sale. However, dozens of rare or endangered plants – from the Lady's Slipper Orchid and Adder's Tongue, to Threadmoss and Sandwort – are protected under the 1981 Wildlife and Countryside Act and to pick them is strictly forbidden. NEVER uproot the whole plant when you pick.

If in doubt, take a photo rather than pick. The natural world is there for us all to enjoy and why deprive others of the joy of discovering something beautiful?

Choose trails in valleys or on sunny, south-facing slopes, both of which are likely to have the best combination of sun and rain in which plant-life blooms.

FLY ORCHID

Timing is everything. Plants generally start to bloom as early as March or April in southern spots, and May and June further north. A good guideline is to head out before the foliage begins to completely shade the ground.

Time your visit after the rain, especially in drier areas. You will find the number and diversity of wildflowers is greatly improved.

Dress for the outdoors: insect repellent, suncream, warm clothing. As ever, be mindful of the environment into which you are venturing.

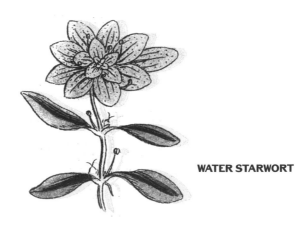

WATER STARWORT

Take a field guide with you – searching for a particular species makes the whole experience more rewarding. The flowers illustrated here are some of the flowers native to our area of the UK. Serious seekers will carry a magnifying glass to inspect the petals and leaves up close as well as a camera to capture what you find.

Grow a 'surprise garden' from the seeds that you collect on your clothing.

Especially if you have been trekking through mud, you will discover a host of seeds stuck to your boots.

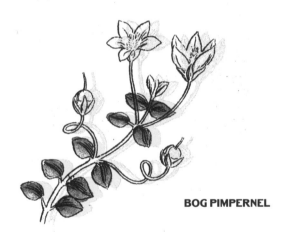

BOG PIMPERNEL

SKIM A STONE

'If it weren't for the rocks in its bed, the stream would have no song'

CARL PERKINS

The Guinness World Record for skims of a stone is an incredible 88. It was set in 2013 by American Kurt Steiner on a lake in Emporium, Pennsylvania. To achieve this remarkable feat, Mr Steiner dedicated his life to the sport, including amassing a collection of 10,000 'quality rocks' in preparation for his ultimate throw.

While you are, frankly, unlikely to get anywhere near Mr Steiner's number of skims, you can significantly increase your personal best (and look cool too) by following a few simple steps.

First of all, you want to find a calm body of water. The calmer it is, the less resistance you will be up against and the better your chances of getting a high number of skims.

Next you need to find the right stone. The consensus here is that you want something flat and oval-shaped that feels the right size in your hand (so it's easy to pick up) and which is neither too heavy nor too light. For what it's worth, Mr Steiner opts for stones weighing 'between 3–8 ounces... that are very smooth (they don't have to be perfectly round), have flat bottoms and are between ¼ – ⁵⁄₁₆ th an inch thick'.

There is some disagreement, though, on the ideal texture you want to find.

Most experts (and believe it or not, some eminent scientists are interested in the physics of skimming stones, as it has a bearing on things such as how ships stay afloat during storms) seem to think that the smoother, the better. However, others believe that stones with a rough texture are best at countering the air- and water-resistance, as with the dimples on a golf ball.

Whichever type you opt for, once you have settled on the right stone, you want to hold it in your hand with your thumb and first finger out, and rest the stone on your second finger. Looking from above, your hand should look like a backwards 'C' or a 'U', with the stone between your thumb and first finger.

With the stone firmly in place, so that it doesn't wobble, pull your hand and wrist back a bit and then flick them forward, releasing the stone away from you as you do so.

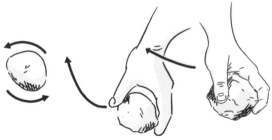

You are aiming to release the stone with as much spin on it as possible. This 'gyroscopic effect' ensures stability according to the same physics as the bullet from a rifle. You also want it to fly at as level a distance from the ground as possible, rather than throwing it up in the air only to arc down into the water. This way, when the stone makes contact with the water it should bounce and skip off the surface. Ideally, the stone should strike the water at an angle of 10–20 degrees.

10–20°/

SKIM A STONE

It can help to crouch down as you throw, to bring your throwing arm and the stone level to the ground as you release. And it can also help to pick a spot on the water where you want the first bounce to land.

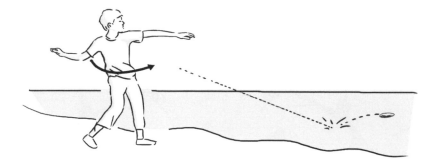

'THE WORLD IS BUT A
CANVAS TO OUR IMAGINATION'

HENRY DAVID THOREAU

LISTEN TO THE DAWN CHORUS

'The earth has music for those who listen'

GEORGE SANTAYANA

During the spring and early summer, it needn't be your alarm clock or the dustbin men that rouse you from sleep. From March to July (in the UK), you are likely to hear the feathered chorus of birds defending their territories and doing their best to attract mates.

Songbirds, or perching birds, account for nearly half of the world's 9,600 species, so no matter where you are you have a chance of catching a good chorus.

Songbirds in much of the northern hemisphere time their breeding season for the warmest part of the year, when food is plentiful and the days are longest. As winter becomes spring, the songbirds (all of which are male) are triggered into breeding mode by the lengthening of the light. At the start of the season you will hear resident birds – robins, great tits – to be joined later by migrants such as blackcaps and chiffchaffs. May and June are thus the best time of year to enjoy the chorus.

To get the fullest experience, you want to begin listening about an hour before sunrise. Often, particular species will begin before others. Robins, blackbirds, skylarks and song thrushes are all early starters, getting to work as soon as the juicy earthworms start to appear, while wrens and warblers will join later, when their insect food source starts to emerge.

Primarily, however, the chorus is a means of attracting a mate and females will use the strength of a particular male's song to identify the best suitor. Once a male has succeeded in finding a mate, he will sing less often. So, if you can hear song late into the season it is likely to be a lonely bachelor!

If you want to enjoy the dawn chorus then the best days are those which are still and with fine weather, when the sound will carry furthest. Remember to take warm clothes to wrap up against the cold weather.

The chorus peaks from half an hour before until half an hour after the sunrise. Painfully early, but it is a magical orchestra with which to begin to the day.

MAKE A DAISY CHAIN

'The Pyramids will not last a moment compared with the daisy.'
DAVID HERBERT LAWRENCE

The name 'daisy' comes from the Old English *'daes eage'*, meaning 'day's eye' - a reference to the way daisies close their petals each evening and open them at the beginning of each new day.

The daisy was originally native to northern Europe but has since been propagated to such an extent that it can be found on every continent except Antarctica.

Widespread as they are, though, daisies are nonetheless remarkable. Their medicinal properties have long been well known – employed to slow bleeding, relieve indigestion and ease coughs, among other ailments. Indeed, the flower's Latin name, *Bellis perennis*, may come from *bellum*, meaning war, because doctors of the Roman army soaked bandages in their juice to bind soldiers' wounds.

Putting their healing properties to one side, when formed into a chain, daisies also make a beautiful garment for a spring or summer's day.

There are two ways of making a chain; the first, which many of us will instantly think of, involves splitting the stems of each daisy to tie them together. The second is more complicated and braids the stems together to create a beautiful object.

SPLIT THE STEMS

Pick daisies with the thickest stems you can find and with fully open flowers for the best effect.

Cut a small slit in the middle of the stem, taking care not to break it in half. You can use your thumbnail or, if you are a chronic nail-biter, a plastic knife will do.

Thread the stem of another daisy through the slit, all the way until the head of the flower is cradled by the slit.

Repeat this until you are ready to close off your crown. To do this, you need to make a slit in the last daisy on the chain about twice the length of the rest. You might want to pluck the flowers from the original daisy to make this easier to pull it through.

BRAIDING A CHAIN

With braiding, the longer the stem the better. The longer and more flexible the stems are, the easier they are to work with.

Take three daisies, strip the leaves from the stems and place all three in a row on a flat surface. Pinch the stems at the top near the flower head.

Bring the right stem over into the middle and press a finger down where the two stems cross over.

Bring the left stem over the new middle stem and beneath the stem on the right. Gently pull all three stems to make it taut, taking extra care not to break them.

WORK OUT A HEDGEROW'S AGE

'Age is not how old you are, but how many years of fun you've had'

MATT MALDRE

Hedgerows are not only one of Britain's most important natural habitats – home to songbirds, mice, shrews and an ecosystem of mammal and insect life – they are also a living piece of our history. Enclosed areas of land marked out by the environment are thought to date as far back the Bronze Age, while they were a favourite of the organisational-minded Romans.

The first living hedgerows, as we know them now, were an invention of the late twelfth century, when King John boosted the royal treasury by leasing assarts (areas of woodland cleared for agriculture) of the Royal Forests.

With a little knowledge and attention to detail, you can trace a hedgerow's history, thanks to a system devised by Dr Max Hooper in the 1970s.

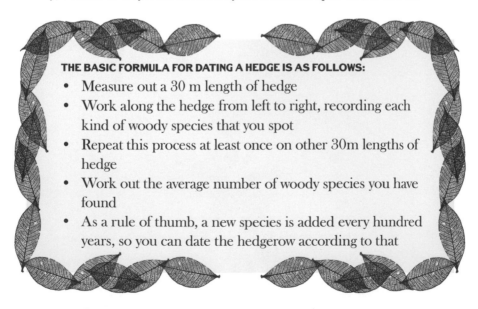

THE BASIC FORMULA FOR DATING A HEDGE IS AS FOLLOWS:

- Measure out a 30 m length of hedge
- Work along the hedge from left to right, recording each kind of woody species that you spot
- Repeat this process at least once on other 30m lengths of hedge
- Work out the average number of woody species you have found
- As a rule of thumb, a new species is added every hundred years, so you can date the hedgerow according to that

Species that you are likely to find in the UK include: hazel, oak, sycamore, beech, bramble and elm, among many others.

HAZEL

ASH

And in between the trees and shrubs there are a whole host of common plants you might spot, many of them with wonderfully eccentric names: hornbeam, bird cherry, goosegrass, rowan, wood sorrel, and guelder rose.

SYCAMORE

PRIMROSE

FERN   **GOOSEGRASS**

MAKE YOUR OWN WALKING STICK

'Depend on your walking stick, not on other people'

JAPANESE PROVERB

'You. Shall. Not. PASS!' OK, we can't all be Gandalf – that takes years of practice and an expert knowledge of sorcery – but nonetheless a good walking stick makes any country ramble that much more pleasant.

And as you steer your way across the fields and dales, it might just help fool onlookers into mistaking you for an experienced woodsman.

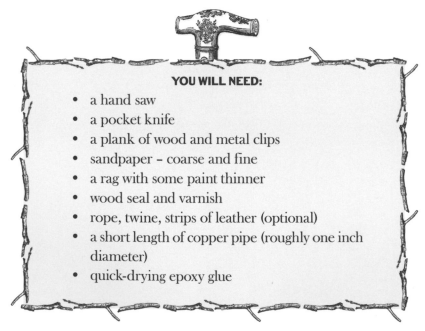

YOU WILL NEED:

- a hand saw
- a pocket knife
- a plank of wood and metal clips
- sandpaper – coarse and fine
- a rag with some paint thinner
- wood seal and varnish
- rope, twine, strips of leather (optional)
- a short length of copper pipe (roughly one inch diameter)
- quick-drying epoxy glue

The first step is to select the best possible piece of wood – size, strength and age are all important. A good walking stick is usually a relatively straight piece of wood of roughly 1–2 inches (2.5 cm–5 cm) in diameter. You want it to be about as tall as your armpit, ideally.

Hardwoods usually make the best walking sticks: aspen, cherry, maple and alder are all good choices.

You want wood that is as fresh as possible but taken from a tree that is no longer living. As with so much else in the wild, you must be respectful of the environment. With a bit of searching, you should be able to find something appropriate.

Don't opt for sticks with holes or insect life in them, as they will be weakened.

MAPLE TREE

Now you need to trim your stick to length. To find the right length, hold the stick as you would when walking, so that your elbow is at a right angle.

Make a mark 2 inches (5 cm) above the top of your hand (allowing more room if you want to add a decorative carving later). Cut it to length using the hand saw, taking great care and keeping away from children.

Next you need to remove the bark. Using the pocket knife, first remove any twigs and bumps from the stick, using short, shallow strokes. You don't want to cut too deep; avoid digging into the wood itself.

Remember always to whittle away from your body, keeping your legs well clear of the action of the knife. Take special care dealing with any knots in the wood, which can cause the knife to skip and could puncture your leg.

You want to whittle until the bright wood beneath the bark shows. There may be more than one layer of bark, so continue until it is all removed.

Now your stick is prepared, it needs time to dry. Wood is 'hygroscopic', meaning that it takes in and lets out water to balance with its environment, so it is naturally moist. While fresh, moist wood is perfect for whittling, it is too soft and flexible to make a good walking stick. Dried wood is both more rigid and durable, so you need some drying time.

The amount of time you will want your stick to dry depends on what type it is, environmental conditions and just how hard you like it to be. Usually, people will wait between two to four weeks.

You want the stick to dry so that it becomes rigid but not brittle. To keep the wood from warping as it dries, a good tip is to pin it to a flat surface, such as a piece of timber, using metal clips (turning it every now and then if necessary). You don't want your wood to dry too quickly, as it can become brittle. So, if it's too warm indoors, opt for a shed or garage instead.

Next you need to personalise your stick – this will make your stick beautiful and individual, but mainly it is so it can be easily identified after a few pints at the local pub. If you have some wood-carving experience, then there is a plethora of tools that you can use to make intricate, expert designs. If not, your trusty pocket knife will do the trick. Remember to take great care and always carve away from your hands and body. As well as design features, ergonomics can be improved by carving grooves for your hand and fingers to make the grip more comfortable. Alternatively, you can apply a leather grip once the stick is complete.

MAKE YOUR OWN WALKING STICK

The final stage for treating the stick is to stain and seal the wood. Like human skin, wood has pores. By sealing the wood, you are closing off these pores and helping your stick to stay strong for a long time to come, as well as making it look even cooler.

Before you seal or stain the wood, use the sandpaper (coarse before fine) to smooth it down. Remove any sawdust using the rag and paint thinner.

Apply the wood stain according to the instructions on the tin, before the varnish. Once dried, use the sandpaper to smooth away any excess. Remember to follow all safety instructions necessary when using the seal and varnish.

If you decided not to carve a handle, then you can wind material around the head of the stick to create a handsome and comfortable grip. Rope, nylon and strips of leather (which look especially smart) are all good options. Use pins or small nails to secure the bound material.

Finally, since the base of your stick is going to see the most wear, it is a good idea to protect it. The best and smartest way of doing this is with a short length of copper pipe. Take a 1 inch (2.5 cm) length of pipe and whittle the base of your stick so that the pipe just fits, before using the glue to affix.

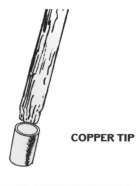

COPPER TIP

YODELLING

'My heart is like a singing bird'

CHRISTINA ROSSETTI

Yodelling is thought to date back at least as far as the 16th-century, when Alpine herders would use it as a call for their livestock. With a sound that carries great distances, the 'herder's cry', as it was known, also came to be used as a means of communication between people – with signature yodels able to identify just who it was doing the distant yelling.

The idea is to switch between the two vocal registers: commonly known as 'head' and 'chest' voices. A good yodeller might change register several times in only a few seconds and at a loud volume – a technique made famous by Tarzan's jungle cry.

And just like Tarzan, yodelling is truly best done in the great outdoors. Not only because you will feel more like a Swiss herder but also because your neighbours will thank you for it.

The trick to yodelling is to find the break in your voice: the point where your lower 'chest' voice switches into the higher pitch 'head' voice.

This break in your voice is created by your epiglottis – a flap at the back of your tongue whose main job is to stop you choking on food.

Begin practising with just one sound – for instance, 'OH' – and try to move from low to high notes. Once you can do that, try switching from a low 'OH' to a high sound 'OU'. You don't want the notes to slide together smoothly – the idea is to have a distinct break between notes.

Next, you are ready for what's known as a 'triad yodel', a sound formed of three notes. Try singing the notes A E and D. Once you can do that, you can add in the word 'yodel' to sing 'Yodel A E D!'

DOWSING

'If you want to find the secrets of the universe, think in terms of energy, frequency and vibration' **NIKOLA TESLA**

Dowsing is officially classed as a 'pseudoscience', meaning (depending on your view) that is either a science in all but name or a load of old codswallop. The idea behind it is that a dowsing (also known as 'divining') rod can be used to find various interesting things hidden beneath the earth – most commonly ground water, but buried metals, gemstones, oils, ores and even gravesites have all supposedly been found using this magical practice.

Whatever the case, the Christian church have long considered dowsing an unholy art. In 15th-century Germany, Martin Luther condemned dowsing as an act in breach of the first commandment – i.e. occultism – and it was officially forbidden by the Inquisition in France in the 17th-century, where it had been used to track criminals and heretics.

Nowadays, boring scientific-minded people would say that the motion of dowsing rods is caused by what is known as the 'ideomotor effect': effectively subconscious movements of the body. But perhaps that's much too cynical.

In either case, if you want to have a go at waving a stick and at least giving people the impression that you possess mystical powers, then the simplest way of divining for water is to pick a dowsing rod made from a tree branch.

The classic divining rod consists of a 'Y'-shaped branch, which can be taken from a tree or a bush. The branch needs to be at least a foot long (30 cm) and you want the two forks to be roughly the same length, so your rod is balanced. Remember that if you believe there are mystical forces at work that enable a branch to detect energy lines, then you probably also believe that trees have spiritual energy: so don't go around blindly plucking branches.

Be deliberate in your choice of branch and consider leaving something of your own in return for this gift from nature.

Many dowsers prefer their branches to be freshly cut, rather than using dead wood from the ground, and hazel and witch hazel are favourite donor trees. Light and porous as they are, it is believed that the wood from these trees is most receptive to the vapours that rise from hidden water sources and buried metals, which weigh down the un-forked end of your rod and point it towards the object.

Simply hold one fork in each hand and point the rod away from you at an arm's length. The fork should be parallel with the ground or tilted very slightly downward.

Wait for the rod to point and, hey presto, you have made your discovery!

FIVE TREES YOU SHOULD KNOW

'Time spent among trees is never wasted time'
KATRINA MAYER

I f it weren't enough that trees are crucial to sustaining life on our planet, they are also central to the story of humankind. Here are five trees worth getting to know.

CHESTNUT
Castanea sativa
Native to southern Europe, western Asia and north Africa.

HOW TO SPOT THEM:
Mature chestnut trees can grow up to 35 m tall and the longest-living examples are 700 years old. They have a smooth greyish-purple bark, with vertical fissures that appear with age.

Look for oblong, toothed leaves with a pointed tip and prominent parallel veins. Chestnuts have long, cylindrical yellow flowers known as catkins and shiny red-brown nuts wrapped in a green, spiky case.

INTERESTING FACT:
For the two years Anne Frank spent hidden in the annex of her father's workplace, a single attic window was her only view on to the outside world. Anne would often write about the beauty of the single white horse-chestnut tree in the courtyard below her, as she yearned for the freedom of the birds who perched on its branches.

On 23 February 1944, just six months before Anne and all those with her were arrested, she wrote a poignant entry in her diary:

'The two of us [Peter van Pels and Anne] looked out at the blue sky, the bare chestnut tree glistening with dew, the seagulls and other birds glinting with silver as they swooped through the air, and we were so moved and entranced that we couldn't speak.'

Sadly, the tree was lost to a storm in 2010. However, its chestnuts were used to germinate saplings that have since been planted around the world, thus ensuring that the tree, and Anne Frank's legacy, live on.

APPLE
Malus x domestica

There are an incredible 7,500 types of apple around the world, each with a unique set of qualities that make them variously best eaten raw, cooked or used to make cider.

HOW TO SPOT THEM:
Apples are small- to medium-sized trees, growing up to 10 m in height. Look for dark green leaves, typically oval-shaped with serrated edges and furred undersides. The bark is usually grey in colour, with bumps, ridges and scales.

The apple tree's flowers are five-petalled and white with hints of pink, growing in clusters known as blossoms.

INTERESTING FACT:
According to a story first spread by Isaac Newton himself to friends and early biographers, it was while resting in the garden of his childhood home in Woolsthorpe Manor, on a summer's day in 1666, that he was struck by an apple falling from a tree.

This was said to have been the inspiration that led him to his scientific breakthrough into the laws of gravitation.

The tree remains there to this day. Although it blew down in 1820, it has since regrown, in its own quiet defiance of gravity.

OAK
Quercus robur

English oak is a large, deciduous tree that can grow up to 40 m tall. As oaks mature, they form broad, spreading crowns with sturdy branches beneath.

This relatively open canopy lets through a good deal of light, meaning that primroses and bluebells often grow in the dappled shade beneath.

HOW TO SPOT THEM:

Oaks have smooth, silvery-brown bark that becomes deeply fissured with age, like old skin. Its leaves are around 10 cm long with 4 or 5 deep lobes and smooth edges and it flowers with long yellow catkins.

The oak tree's acorns are green at first, before ripening into brown and falling from their stalks on to the ground.

INTERESTING FACT:

The oak is one of the most celebrated and revered trees in the history of civilisation. It was sacred to the Greeks (Zeus), the Romans (Jupiter) and the Celts (Dagda) – all of whom associated their gods of thunder with this woodland lightning rod.

Druids considered them sacred and would practise their rites in oak groves. British royals have also long been fans - for a long time adorning themselves in crowns made from the oak's leaves. Charles II is said to have escaped his Roundhead pursuers by hiding in an oak tree after things went wrong at the Battle of Worcester in 1651.

FIG

Ficus carica

Fig trees are among the first plants to have been cultivated by humans and for that reason are enshrined perhaps more than any other in mythology and theology, from the fig leaves that covered Adam and Eve to the tree under which Romulus and Remus were suckled by wolves.

Native to the Middle East and western Asia, they have since been naturalised in parts of Asia and North America and there are now more than 700 named types.

HOW TO SPOT THEM:

Fig trees grow up to 10 metres tall and have beautifully fragrant leaves that grow to about 12–25 centimetres (5–10 inches) in length.

The fig's 'fruit' is not strictly speaking a fruit at all. It is a 'false fruit', a part of the stem of the tree that becomes a fleshy bag for flowers and seeds. Whether fruit or not, the fig has been a staple of countless civilisations, including the ancient Greeks, who considered them so essential they banned them from being exported.

INTERESTING FACT:

Brought to Sri Lanka in the 3rd-century BC, the Jaya Sri Maha Bodi, better known as the 'Bodhi Tree', is said to be the oldest tree with a known planting date. This sacred fig tree is recognised by Buddhists as a branch of the original tree under which Buddha first gained enlightenment.

According to Buddhist texts, the Buddha meditated under this tree without leaving his seat for seven days. A shrine, called Animisalocana Cetiya, was later erected on the spot where he sat.

A separate sacred fig at the Mahabodhi Temple in Bodh Gaya, India, is also said to be a direct descendant of the Buddha's original tree.

REDWOOD
Sequioadendron giganteum

The redwood is the largest and tallest species of tree in the world, reaching an incredible 380 feet tall and capable of living for thousands of years.

Redwoods are wrapped in bark that grows up to 12 inches thick, and its branches can reach up to 5 feet in diameter.

HOW TO SPOT THEM:
As its nickname suggests, giant or coastal redwoods thrive in the moist, humid climate of the northern california coast, where marine fog delivers the precise conditions needed for its growth.

The fog adds moisture to the soil and helps trap it there by lowering the rate of evaporation.

INTERESTING FACT:
The world's tallest known living tree is a redwood named 'Hyperion'.

Towering almost 380 feet above Redwood National and State Parks in California, this record-breaking tree was discovered in 2006 by amateur naturalists who named it after the Titan of Greek mythology, appropriately the child of Gaia, goddess of the Earth, and Uranus, god of the sky.

Hyperion's exact location is kept secret for its own protection. And with good reason: the area was once home to thousands of redwoods of Hyperion's size, before the devastating impact of logging left this magnificent being towering alone.

MAKE YOUR OWN BEE HOUSE

'The keeping of bees is like the direction of sunlight'
HENRY DAVID THOREAU

The world's bee population is under serious threat. And it is not merely bees: the number of 'pollinators' in the world – a group of about 20,000 flying species essential to the reproduction of plant life – is shrinking rapidly. No one is sure exactly why, because there are so many potential factors: global warming, pesticides, loss of habitat and disease.

What is clear, though, is that it is our own future as a species that is also at stake.

The world's food supply depends on crops, and crops exist only because of pollination. With bees, butterflies and some species of bird facing extinction, there are scary times ahead if we don't begin to make some changes.

While the United Nations tackle that problem, you can play your own part in the restoration of bee-kind by building a simple bee house

YOU WILL NEED

1. Pencil
2. Sticky tape
3. Bamboo canes
4. Hollow plant stems or reeds
5. Chunks of untreated hardwood or logs
6. Offcuts of planks of wood 1.5 cm thick
7. Saw
8. Nails
9. Drill
10. Brown paper

THE STRUCTURE

Simply put, you need to either make or buy a box stuffed full of different-sized hollow tubes. Each tube will need to be roughly 15 cm (6 inches) long and have one dead end.

You can be creative with your materials and designs but the important thing is that your bee house is solid enough to survive outdoors for years.

MAKING YOUR BEE HOUSE

Take a plank of timber roughly 1–2 cm (½–¾ inch) thick and cut it into the shapes shown in the diagram to make a box of three compartments.

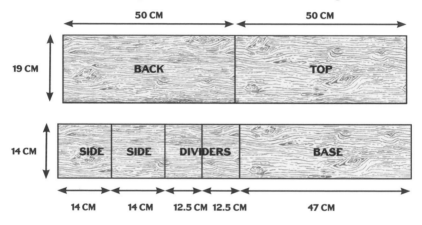

Use the hammer and nails to join it together. It must be at least 20 cm (8 inches) deep and the roof needs a decent overhang to protect your house from the rain. Depending on your woodwork skills, you can either turn the roof vertically or make it pitched.

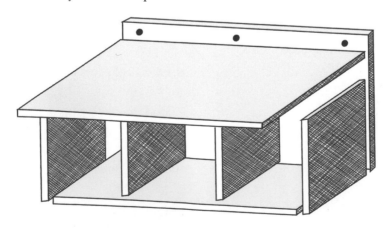

NOTE: *The dimensions given here are for 10 mm-thick wood. If your wood is a different size then the dimensions of the base should be 500 mm minus 2 x the thickness of the wood, and the side pieces should be 125 mm + thickness of wood.*

MAKING THE NESTING TUBES

You can buy ready-made bee tubes, but you can also simply make them from the dead stems of hollow plants and reeds. First, cut the tubes to 10 cm (4") length. You also want to drill deep holes of varying sizes (5–10 mm in diameter) into blocks of wood and logs, again about 10 cm (4") deep.

Fill your box with your tubes and blocks of wood, packing the tubes tightly together so they stay put.

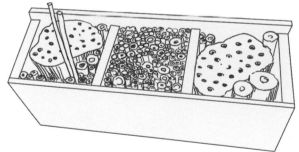

POSITIONING THE BEE HOUSE

Fix the box to a fence or wall securely at roughly chest height. Crucially, you need to place it facing south in a sunny position, if possible near to flowers and plants.

Now watch for visiting bees. Adult female bees will visit the nestholes on sunny days during spring and summer. You might notice them flying in ferrying pollen or bits of mud, which they will use to create cell walls along the tube, or with bits of leaf.

Holes that are in use will be blocked with plugs of mud or leaves. Mother bees will lay eggs in those cells, leaving their young a food supply of pollen and nectar. The bee grubs will then grow up in their tubes and hatch the following year, meaning you have helped to guarantee at least one more generation of the species.

MAKE YOUR OWN BEE HOUSE

GRASS WHISTLE

'You never get an angry man suddenly breaking into a whistle'

KARL PILKINGTON

Nature produces many glorious sounds: the rustle of leaves in the autumn breeze, the percussive murmur of waves crashing on the shore, the gentle lowing of cattle. And now you can make your own contribution to this natural orchestra – albeit with a sound more like a rather unfortunate squawk than anything else – simply by blowing on a blade of grass.

First, choose a blade that is at least 3 inches long and as wide as possible – if it has a seam running down the middle then that is a good sign, as it means it's nice and wide. The tougher the grass, the better too.

Place the blade against the outside edge of one of your thumbs - i.e. the side furthest from your fingers – and press the outside edge of your other thumb up against it. It helps to begin with the fleshy bottom part of your thumb and rock up towards the tip. The idea is to have your thumbs pressed side by side with a small gap naturally formed in between, in which the blade is held taut, mimicking the reed in a wind instrument.

Press your lips to the gap and blow. It helps if you try making a small slit between your lips. This should produce a surprisingly loud buzzing sound. By moving the tips of your thumbs backwards and forwards, you can alter the tension of the blade and shift the pitch.

BAMBOO WIND CHIMES

'Surround yourself with the music of life and you cannot help
but sing its song' **SUE KREBS**

Though you might not at first think so, wind chimes are in fact musical instruments and an example of what is known as 'chance-based music'. The difference is that they draw on the random movement of air, rather than human skill, to create melodies and broken chords. They are also, as with so many things, much older than you might realise, dating back at least as far as ancient Rome, where the tinkling of bronze chimes was believed to ward off evil spirits.

In China, glass wind chimes were hung from the corners of temples, palaces and the roofs of homes because they bring good fortune according to Feng Shui.

Whether or not they attract good luck, this set of bamboo chimes provide a beautifully melodic backdrop to time spent outside and is something you can make with tools at home.

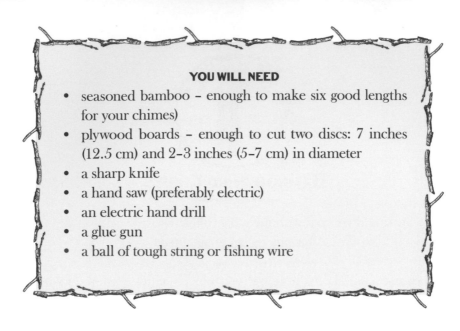
You might be fortunate enough to live in an area where bamboo grows naturally, or be able to grow your own, but if not then most garden centres will have a plentiful supply of bamboo of various sizes.

You need bamboo that is well-seasoned (dried) and without any splits or rot. First, you need to cut the bamboo into six lengths, with each length made up of two sections. One end needs to be cut above the partition-like segment end, and the other below it, so you have an open tube to work with.

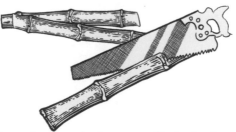

With a sharp knife, make a vertical cut to split the hollow end of each piece. Take great care not to cut yourself with the knife nor the bamboo shards, which can be incredibly sharp.

Taper off the cut at roughly the last inch, so your knife exits at a horizontal angle.

Drill holes just above the section on the solid end of each piece, parallel to the cut you made at the opposite end. This will mean that once assembled the bamboo 'channel' on each tube will be facing inwards.

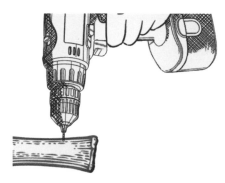

Now, use the hand saw to cut a circle from the plywood approximately six times the diameter of the tubes. In our example, the tubes were roughly 1 inch (2.5 cm) in diameter, so the circle was 6 inches (15 cm).

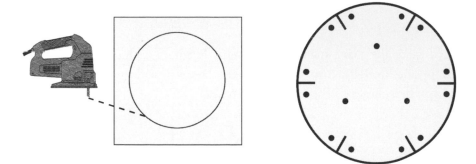

With a ruler, mark six equal spaces around the circumference of the disc before drilling a ⅛ inch (4 mm) hole on both sides of each mark, roughly ¾ inch (2 cm) to either side, and roughly the same distance from the edge of the disc.

Thread the string through both the holes and make a knot at one end. Each piece of string needs to be roughly 50 inches (1.3 m) long, though you can trim any excess.

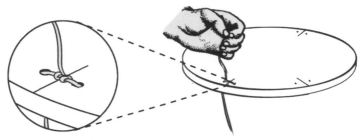

Now thread the other end of the string through the holes in the end of one bamboo section before continuing the thread through the next hole in the disc on the other side of your mark. Repeat this until all the pieces of bamboo are hanging beneath the disc, before tying off the string.

You can slide the string around to adjust the height of each piece of bamboo. This distance from the disc is what changes the tone produced, so experiment until you have a range of sounds that you like.

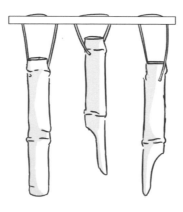

Next, use the drill to make three evenly spaced holes 1–2 inches (roughly 4 cm) from the centre of the disc. Cut three pieces of string 25 inches (60 cm) in length and tie them together at one end to make a little loop.

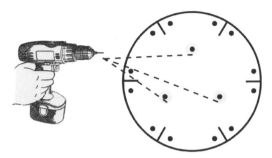

Thread each string through a hole, pulling them taut, and while holding the disc level use the glue gun to apply a dollop of glue to help hold each in place.

Now use the handsaw to cut a smaller disc, 1–2 times the diameter of your bamboo pieces. (In our case, this was roughly 2½ inches.)

Use the hand drill to make three holes of 3–4 mm equally spaced around the disc, roughly an inch (2.5 cm) from the centre.

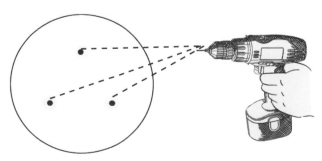

Thread the loose ends of the three centre strings through these holes, so that this disc hangs roughly one-third of the way down from the tops of the bamboo pieces.

Use the glue gun again to fasten these strings to the disc, taking care to keep the smaller disc level as you do so. (This smaller disc will be the percussive that strikes the bamboo pieces and makes your sound.)

Use a small stone or heavy object and tie it on to the end of the strings from the lower disc.

This is going to catch the wind and swing the hammer into the bamboo pieces. Generally speaking, the larger the surface area of this piece, the more your hammer will swing and the more noise your chimes will make.

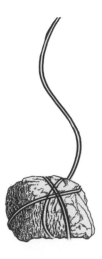

Use the glue gun to fasten any loose ends of string to make sure your chime stays solid in the mellifluous breeze.

Hang your wind chimes somewhere that receives a steady breeze, and sit back and enjoy nature's music.

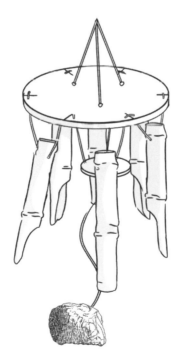

SLACKLINING

'Balance is not something you find, it's something you create'

JANA KINGSFORD

Apparently the 'doing stupid things for fun' gene has been around for some time, as human beings have enjoyed walking precarious ropes for thousands of years. The ancient Greeks are thought to have been the first and the given name is theirs: 'funambulism'. The word owes nothing to 'fun', sadly, but instead comes from the Latin 'funis' for rope and 'ambulare', meaning to walk.

The version of rope walking we know as 'slacklining' is thought to have been invented by Adam Grosowsky. The story goes that Grosowsky, the son of an Illinois university professor, came across a photo in the college library of 19th-century wirewalkers in action and became obsessed.

From that point, he dedicated himself to becoming a master of the art and has spent much of his life since spreading the culture of slacklining.

The point of slacklining versus other types of rope-walking is that is uses flat webbing, instead of wire or rope, which is held with much less tension and as such is much more accessible to the beginner.

A basic slackline is generally anchored between two trees.

You can pick up a slackline from a range of stores and each will come with its own instructions as to how to safely install it, which need to be followed to the letter – not only for your safety but to ensure that no damage is done to the supporting trees.

Great care should be taken if you are considering using man-made fixtures for anchors as objects such as lampposts and fence posts are not designed for lateral force.

With your slackline in place, most experts will say that is best to begin bare-foot, as this allows for better contact with the line. (As you progress to tricks and flips you will need footwear.)

If there is one skill that slacklining requires above all others, it is patience. You are going to fall. A *lot*. So, be positive, enjoy the learning process and keep getting back on that line.

A good idea is to learn to balance on the line before you try to walk it. First, position yourself near the middle of the line and place one foot on it, facing forwards (inline), not across.

Don't press down on the line as it will begin to wobble. Instead, make sure your leg is relaxed. Do this with both legs until you have a good feel for the line.

Once ready, push yourself up to a standing position – still with one leg only – and count to 20, concentrating on balancing.

Bend your knees a little to lower your centre of gravity as well as helping to absorb movement in the line. You will wobble to begin with, but you will quickly learn to adjust for that.

Keep your arms above your head so that your elbows are above your shoulders. This will feel silly to begin with but it's important for your balance.

Do not wave your arms around and do not hold them straight out to the sides like you might have seen in the movies. The point is to be able to shift the weight with your arms and spare leg while balancing.

Your back must be kept straight. Whatever you do, don't lean forwards as this will make you more likely to fall and take uneven steps.

Crucially, don't look straight down but instead focus on something a little way in front of you along the line.

NOW YOU ARE READY TO LEARN TO WALK
Keep your position as above with your feet inline and your head, chest and hips straight (i.e. flat against the anchor). If the line begins to swing, lower your centre of gravity by further bending your knees.

If you feel yourself losing balance, as you certainly will, try to stay on the line for as long as you can. Every moment spent on the line will help you to build muscle memory.

You can make things easier by having a friend sit on the other end of the line to make it more stable.

Once you have mastered walking, you can attempt some basic skills. Turning around, walking backwards and jumping are excellent show-off pieces with which to begin.

'NOT UNTIL WE ARE LOST
DO WE BEGIN TO FIND OURSELVES'

HENRY DAVID THOREAU

CROP CIRCLES

'No object is mysterious. The mystery is your eye'

ELIZABETH BOWEN

Variously attributed to pranksters, alien visitors and even witchcraft, crop circles have had people scratching their heads, and farmers jumping up and down in fury, for centuries.

The first sighting is thought to have been as long ago as 1678, in a gloriously named publication called *The Mowing-Devil, or Strange News out of Hert-fordshire*. This woodcut pamphlet told the story of a farmer so incensed by the price a labourer had quoted him to mow his field that he declared he would rather it were done by the Devil himself. That night, he awoke to find his fields aflame and by the next morning they were perfectly mowed.

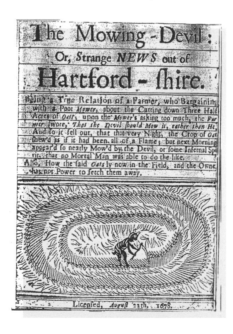

This is considered by many cereologists to be the first account of a crop circle (although in this case the crops were cut rather than flattened) but there have been many more over the centuries, with a particular resurgence in the late 20th-century.

Crop circles are now recognised by almost everyone not to be caused by UFOs or anything so exciting but instead the work of dedicated pranksters. The fact that they were thought for so long to be other-worldly and supernaturally complex, though, is a testament to the skill and artistry that goes into creating them.

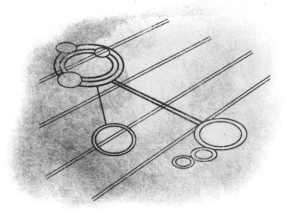

The important point is that making crop circles on fields that don't belong to you or for which you don't have permission is vandalism. So, before you do anything, you must make sure that you have the right authority or you could break the law and face a hefty fine.

Most crop circles are created by teams, so you will want to gather some friends.

Traditionally most crop circles have been made at night, under the cover of darkness, but given that you won't be doing anything illegal you will have the benefit of being able to see what you are doing.

The first thing you need to do is create your pattern. Most crop artists use computers to help them but you can just as well use pen and ink. Taking inspiration from magnetic fields and other mathematical phenomena found in nature will lend your pattern a suitably authentic and mystical quality.

CROP CIRCLES

You will need: a good amount of string, rope or tape to measure out distances; a lawn roller can be useful for the job of flattening; some wooden stakes to drive into the ground; and most importantly wooden planks of roughly 5 feet (1.5 m) in length, with ropes attached at each end. If possible, use planks of different sizes to create variation.

For what it's worth, rapeseed, barley and wheat are considered the best crops to work with. An important point throughout the process is to try to only walk on those parts that have already been flattened. The best crop circles appear as though they have magically appeared from above, so any footprints leading to and from them are going to ruin the effect.

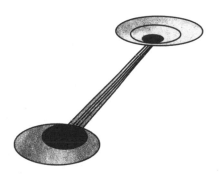

It is a good idea to begin with the centre of your crop pattern and work outwards from there. Start with driving a wooden spike into the centre point as an anchor and attach a rope with which to measure out your first circle.

The traditional way to flatten the crop is to loop the pieces of string tied to the ends of the plank over your shoulders, one on each side, so that as you walk you are pressing the planks down into the crop. Walk in a shuffling motion, so you are continually pressing the crop as you move forward.

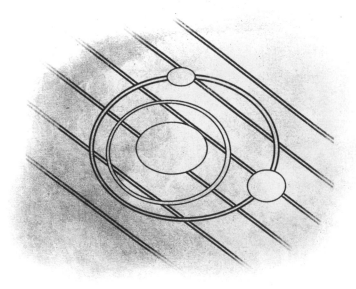

You may want to bend all the crops in a given pattern in the same direction, as the angle of the sunlight striking a crop will affect how it looks – just as it does when you mow the stripes on your lawn. However, once you get the hang of it you can try flattening in different directions to play with lighting effects.

A good place to start is with concentric circles and then an arrangement of circles according to a geometric formation. You can then graduate to using partial circles with overlapping arcs to create interesting effects.

Use a mixture of circles, lines, dots and dashes to create your other-worldly pattern and remember: cover your tracks!

CROP CIRCLES

HOW TO PAINT A WATERCOLOUR LANDSCAPE

'Keep your love of nature, for that is the true way to understand
art more and more'

VINCENT VAN GOGH

There is perhaps no other artist who saw art and nature as so inseparably linked as Van Gogh. A tormented soul, the quiet of the countryside offered him a rare chance of peace. As a child, he would take long walks through the countryside of Brabant, in the Netherlands, and it was here that he developed a life-long love of the natural world.

'In the evening, when we rode back from Zundert over the heath, Pa and I walked a way, the sun set red behind the pines and the evening sky was reflected in the marshes, the heath and the yellow and white and grey sand were so resonant with tone and atmosphere.'

For Van Gogh, the natural world offered the richest source of inspiration to the artistic mind, and there is undoubtedly something magical about turning your eye to a landscape and trying to capture something of its essence.

Here are some tips to set you on your way to bringing the natural world to life on the canvas.

We chose to work with watercolours. If you have some artistic experience already then you might want to work with acrylics on canvas, but for the sake of getting out into the wild and getting down to it, watercolours are easy to work with and require fewer materials.

YOU WILL NEED:

A decent sketch pad

A soft pencil

A set of watercolours

A set of paint brushes

Before you begin, make sure you have plenty of paint mixed and ready to go, as you want to work quickly and not have to pause.

A good place to begin is by drawing the line of the horizon with your pencil and then starting to paint your sky. Notice the range of colours: not just blues but reds, yellows and beyond. Use a large mop brush and move quickly across the page – you are aiming to capture the general impression at this point rather than finer details.

Leave some white paper where required, where the sun is catching in particular. Use grey and red to capture the darker underside of clouds. Notice that where your paint meets paint it will create softer edges, while paint that meets a white paper background will leave a harder edge. This mix of edges is integral to a watercolour scene.

With your sky roughly in place, use your pencil to sketch in the important details in your scene – trees, boats, buildings, whatever they might be. Next, paint in your background, which might be rolling fields or sea or forest, depending on where you are.

The thicker your mix of paint, the stronger your colours will be. Bear this in mind as you paint the main object in your picture. Don't be afraid to go dark from the first time – this will look better than layering multiple washes of paint to build up tone. Paint your object and the shadows they cast at the same time, so they are on the same plane. Another good tip is to use as few brush strokes as possible to paint in any details.

Next paint any objects in the immediate foreground (closest to your eye). Don't worry too much about capturing detail so much as the colours and impression they make.

You can then add marks to suggest detail – footprints in the sand, flowers in a meadow, etc. – using dots, drybrush marks (made by dragging a brush quickly on its side), and a small amount of spatter. Spattering is where you cast spots of paint from your brush by tapping it against your other hand while holding it over the paper. Less is more here.

Now you have the basic order of your painting, here are the top tips to have in mind as you paint:

LIGHT AND DARK

The composition of your landscape painting is first and foremost about capturing the interplay of dark and light. You want to convey to your viewer which aspects of your scene are in light, which are in shade, which are lighter and which are darker. This is known as 'value distribution'. The eye is trained to recognise how natural light is distributed, so if you get this right your painting will instantly have a trueness to it.

The lightest aspect of your painting will be the sky (assuming you are painting during the day), because it is bathed in light. After that comes the 'horizontal', meaning the ground and the horizontal surfaces, which catch and reflect a lot of light. Slightly less light than that are the diagonal surfaces – the roofs and slopes that capture some but not all of the light. And finally the vertical elements – trees trunks, for instance – which capture the least of the sun's reflected light.

THE RELATIONSHIP BETWEEN LIGHT AND COLOUR

A sunny day will make colours more vibrant, warmer and intense. (Similarly, an overcast day will produce more muted colours.) The sun not only lightens colours but adds the yellow tinge of its rays too. So, when painting leaves, grasses or hills that are bathed in light, concentrate on capturing the unique colour of the light falling on them. This might not always be yellow, but blue, red or other colours, depending on the quality of the light.

Recognising the light in your scene will add realism, atmosphere and harmony to your painting.

THE INFLUENCE OF THE ATMOSPHERE

The air is made up of particles that turn the light greyer and lighter. The further the distance an object or scene is from you, the more atmosphere there will be in between, and this will affect the colours of what you are seeing. This is known as 'atmospheric perspective'.

So, objects nearest to you – trees, bushes, etc. – will appear sharpest and darkest, while those nearer the horizon are greyer and lighter.

Use a watered-down mix of greys, blues and whichever darker shades best suit, to create this feeling of haze.

BE SELECTIVE

Landscape painting is all about selecting what to include and what to leave out. With such a vast natural scene to draw on, you need first to decide what your focus will be. Pick a focal point in the landscape. Next you need to choose what size of canvas will best serve the scene and place your focal point accordingly.

Then choose what you are going to include and (more importantly) what you are going to leave out. Simplify – eliminate anything that isn't essential to your picture. Whether you are painting *in situ* or from a photograph, ignore anything you feel won't add to the painting: road signs, paths, livestock. You can also move things around, if necessary. The most important consideration is not realism but getting the best composition.

LAYER AND OVERLAP

Contrasting the shade or texture of two objects can help you to create that all-important sense of depth in your painting. Include objects that overlap and partially obstruct each other to give the viewer the impression of being able to walk into your scene.

AN INTERESTING FOREGROUND

Capturing only things that are in the medium to far distance runs the risk of a flat and lifeless painting. To give your painting a feeling of depth, include an object of interest in the foreground. This will draw the viewer's eye into the scene. For a sense of realism, include less detail and texture for those objects in the background versus those nearest to you.

VARIATION IN SIZE

It may sound obvious, but things get smaller the further they are from you. A dynamic change in size of repeated objects, e.g. a line of trees, creates a powerful impression of depth in your painting.

First published in Great Britain in 2017 by Trapeze
an imprint of The Orion Publishing Group Ltd
Carmelite House, 50 Victoria Embankment
London EC4Y 0DZ

An Hachette UK Company

1 3 5 7 9 10 8 6 4 2

A CIP catalogue record for this book is
available from the British Library.

ISBN 978 1 4091 7272 7
ISBN (eBook) 978 1 4091 7393 9

Printed in Italy

www.orionbooks.co.uk

FSC
www.fsc.org
MIX
Paper from
responsible sources
FSC® C023419